Book Two
On a Wing and a Prayer series

Staying Aloft

*True stories about men
and the extraordinary birds
who loved them!*

Linda Franklin

TEACH Services, Inc.
P U B L I S H I N G
www.TEACHServices.com • (800) 367-1844

World rights reserved. This book or any portion thereof may not be copied or reproduced in any form or manner whatever, except as provided by law, without the written permission of the publisher, except by a reviewer who may quote brief passages in a review.

The author assumes full responsibility for the accuracy of all facts and quotations as cited in this book. The opinions expressed in this book are the author's personal views and interpretations, and do not necessarily reflect those of the publisher.

This book is provided with the understanding that the publisher is not engaged in giving spiritual, legal, medical, or other professional advice. If authoritative advice is needed, the reader should seek the counsel of a competent professional.

Copyright © 2019 Linda Franklin
Copyright © 2019 TEACH Services, Inc.
ISBN-13: 978-1-4796-0939-0 (Paperback)
ISBN-13: 978-1-4796-0940-6 (ePub)
Library of Congress Control Number: 2018913341

True stories about men and the extraordinary birds who loved them!

Edited by Linda Marie Harrington Steinke.

Scriptures are taken from the King James Version of the Bible. Public domain.

Illustrated by Duncan Long.

Published by

TEACH Services, Inc.
P U B L I S H I N G
www.TEACHServices.com • (800) 367-1844

Other books by Linda Franklin

On a Wing and a Prayer series

Book One: *Just a Little Higher*—Comfort comes on soft little wings just when these women need it most!

Book Three: *Climbing the Heights*—Never before published true and inspirational bird stories.

Book Four: *Such Sweet Songs*—Listen carefully! The song of a bird can heal a wounded heart!

Rainbow series

Book One: *Rainbow in the Flames*—A tragic fire, a bow of promise, a love of the lasting kind. The healing journey of an optimistic burn survivor (color photos).

Book Two: *Shadows Point to Rainbows*—The remarkable journey of a devoted dog and his beloved boy.

Book Three: *Johnny Sundown*—A wild trapper discovers solace in Canada's Peace Country.

Survival series

Book One: *Country in My Heart*—Success stories of people who prayed for a country home. Compiled and edited by Jere and Linda Franklin (b/w photos).

Dedication

This book is affectionately dedicated to my father,

Calvin Gordon Harper

who, like every good soldier, stood faithfully at his post.

Contents

Stories

Poems

To the Reader

I am excited to be able to share the stories of these brave men and boys, an elite few, who have been privileged to know ordinary birds in extraordinary ways. Those who share their experiences in this book—trapper, soldier, hunter, psychologist, preacher, repairman, farmer, carpenter, firefighter...from little boys to elderly grandfathers—received a greater respect for themselves, their fellow beings, and their Creator through these close, unexpected, amazing encounters.

The affection shown by the birds in these stories was divinely ordained; the veil of fear replaced with a mantle of trust. What heaven-sent lessons can be learned from the gentle songsters that we take for granted? Have you ever felt the thrill of a friendly chickadee or a saucy little humming-bird perch on your finger? The opportunity of being singled out by one special bird, discerning a new language, becoming sensitive to its lesson, is pure joy!

An eagle's nest full of thanks to the creative individuals who allowed me to share their stories and to those who helped me edit their precious encounters.

A note to those of you who have come to appreciate the little aeronautical angels among us: please send me your bird story! I would love to hear about your encounter. Between the two of us, maybe we can help to give a few more people eyes to see and ears to hear!

Linda Franklin
PO Box 840
Chetwynd, BC V0C 1J0
Canada

Introduction

*I*t's World War II. A midair collision over North Africa wings a B-17. As the wounded war bird falls earthward, pilot Kendrick "Sonny" Bragg clings desperately to the controls of his *All American*, knowing only too well that it will take much more than his accumulated flying skills to safely land his mortally wounded fighter and preserve the lives of his crew. Each breath is a prayer. Miraculously, the injured craft lands safely in a field not far from the First American Squadron's jungle runway. The *All American* becomes a legend.

Back home, his song-writing friends, Jimmy McHugh and Harold Adamson, team up to immortalize one line of Sonny's letter home after that memorable landing—"We came in on one engine and a prayer." The song is soon on the lips of every American who knows, admires, or wants to be a hero.

> *With our full crew aboard,*
> *And our trust in the Lord,*
> *We're comin' in on a wing and a prayer.*
> *Tho' there's one motor gone, we can still carry on...*
> *Comin' in on a wing and a prayer.*

My father longed to be a pilot during WWII, but was informed that his typing skills were sorely needed at a remote jungle outpost near Calcutta,

India to help establish what was later dubbed the "China Burma India Theatre" (CBI). Though he never would divulge details, he did reveal that he served as a liaison between General Hap Arnold at the Pentagon and General Claire Chenault's Flying Tigers in southeast China.

In August of 1945, when Daddy received word of the birth, and subsequent death, of his firstborn son, he was denied his request for leave.

"Stand by your post, Harper!" barked his commanding officer. "Your captain needs you!"

With a limp salute, Daddy stumbled out of the portable office, into the jungle where he collapsed beneath a banyan tree. The raucous parrots and jungle monkeys were uncharacteristically quiet that day, reverencing his private war. For the sake of freedom, Daddy stood by his post; he "held the line" with an old manual typewriter as his weapon, its well-worn keys as ammunition.

It seemed to me that Daddy knew everything there was to know about India. Holding a bronze figurine he brought back from Bombay, he recalled numerous scenes, sorry that his camera had been confiscated lest any war news accidentally fall into the wrong hands. He told us about the acrid smells burning vats of Calcutta, the lepers, orphans, beggars.

The soldiers were exposed to unfamiliar wildlife. Daddy told of the twenty-foot python that was killed with a bow and arrow above his bed in the jungle bunkhouse and how the men always dumped their boots out every morning to insure against being bitten by a baby cobra. He laughed as he told of his bunkmate telling him about running into a gorilla in the dark, only to discover, at sunup, that he was "choked" by clothesline!

I would closely inspect Daddy's souvenirs, trying my best to see a reflection of a Flying Tiger such as he could see in the surfaces of the hand-crafted Indian brass. I admired Daddy's connection to the preservation of freedom. He never allowed the four of his children to forget the troops who sacrificed their hopes, dreams, and lives. And he never lost his love for the glories of flight. When the Blue Angels came to Portland, he'd take the four of us to the airport to watch their daring maneuvers, naming the flight patterns, critical air speed, even the amount of fuel needed. He seemed to experience the same exhilarating freedom as the pilots themselves. I enjoyed watching the Blue Angels, but I always covered my ears, feeling more affinity for the quieter, smaller living birds than for the big, noisy silver war birds he admired.

Daddy held aircraft in high esteem from his early teens. He built a whole roomful of model planes of all sizes and shapes, painting them in minute detail while memorizing flight details of each one. By silhouette, he could recognize any WWII aircraft in a second. Although he never got to fly during the war, he shook the hands of fighter pilots who gave their lives in the turbulent fight for freedom.

As the strength of the eagle's wing, so the vigor of the human spirit is proven in tumultuous times. When Daddy married his high-school sweetheart (my mother) and went off to war, he did not know the price he would pay for his share of "the line" in the CBI Theatre, but it just may have made a difference in the outcome of the war. As painful as their battles were, my parents were stronger for the storms. It made a difference in our lives. We four children learned how to "hold the line," though we never felt the full blast of the tempests that (I would later learn) threatened our home. Mamma and Daddy, trusted, like pilot Sonny Bragg, that they could weather the gale, *"...still carry on...our trust in the Lord, comin' in on a wing and a prayer."* Seeing them face the storm, we learned to appreciate the strength of the human spirit.

Story time was the cement of our childhood dreams and resolutions. When Mamma visited shut-ins or worked a night shift, Daddy filled in with his own experiences in India, reciting Colonel McRae's, *Flanders Fields* from memory, or reading Rudyard Kipling's *Rikki Tikki Tavi, Gunga Din*, or Captain Eddie Rickenbacker's, *We Thought We Heard the Angels Sing*. He narrated inspirational poems to us such as *High Flight* by John Gillespie McGee, Jr. if there was a life-flight lesson therein.

Oh, I have slipped the surly bonds of earth
And danced on laughter-silver wings;
Sunward I've climbed and joined the tumbling mirth
Of sun-split clouds—and done a hundred things
You have not dreamed of—wheeled and soared and flung
My eager craft through footless halls of air.
Up, up the delirious, burning blue
I've topped the wind-swept height with easy grace,
Where never lark or even eagle flew;
And while, with silent, lifting mind I've trod
The high unsurpassed sanctity of space,
Put out my hand, and touched the face of God.

Daddy is not the only one who favors the belief that WWII was "won in the air." Because of the invention of planes, many more lives have been saved than have been lost. How did man learn to fly?—by studying birds. Even very recently, by closely observing the upturned wing tip of soaring birds such as eagles, buzzards, and storks, aeronautical engineers perfected the new "winglet" design to counteract drag on jet wings, saving billions of gallons of fuel in their first year of use.

I studied flight, too. When I raised canaries, I not only learned to admire their flying skills, but their songs, their tenacity and their tenderness as well. Customers shared several inspiring stories about their bird experiences before I began recording them. I perceived a consistent theme. Were some of these visits top-secret flight maneuvers or divine marching orders? Could birds be used by God to help someone "under fire" win a personal battle? With this theory as a premise, I began asking my storyteller friends, "And what was happening in your life when this bird came to you?" Most often "their bird" served as an inspiration during a time of desperate need. Just as the silver birds of WWII pushed back the enemy, could these little angels swoop in as reinforcements, spirit-lifters, inspiration to keep pressing on? No matter what war or rumor thereof might cause us to tremble, the most important battles are still won in the air (Ephesians 6:12)! And God is still in control of every little thing, even the birds.

After establishing the truth of my premise, that birds are definitely used to stir and lift the human spirit, I formed an insatiable appetite to capture these stories so that others might be inspired. The more I hear and write, the more convinced I am that, as He did in Bible times, God is still using birds to speak to us. There are numerous Bible examples, parables and messages about birds. There are stories about specific birds that helped people significantly; Noah's little dove must have struggled hard to bring him some tangible hope with that olive leaf; Elijah was nourished and encouraged by ravens in his wilderness experience during a time of famine; a dove descended from heaven and alighted on Jesus as he arose from baptismal waters to help John recognize and proclaim Him as the long-awaited Messiah.

I like to think of the stories in this book as times when, like a war bird on a mission, a special set of fragile but formidable wings, urged a soldier to "hold the line," and gain an unexpected victory, *on a wing and a prayer.*

Linda Franklin writes from the Peace Country of Northern British Columbia, Canada.

Big Motor

Now we see only puzzling reflections in a mirror,
but then we shall see face to face.

—I Corinthians 13:12 (NEB)

*T*he wilderness had left its mark on John Terry. Living alone in Canada's far North, John was about as tough as they come; he had survived the harshest conditions that weather and circumstance could throw at him. We were warned by more than one person not to take a chance on befriending the "Mad Trapper of the Wolverine." Thankfully, our forty year association with John was symbiotic; we needed each other in diverse ways. Being environmentally connected, John quite naturally shared his apprehension with me when one of his extraordinary animal friends failed to arrive. A most memorable message emerged.

"Whatever you do, don't go visit that mad trapper!" A cattle rancher warned my husband, Jere, the first time we spoke to friends about our intent to visit John Terry.

"He'll pull a rifle on you—quick as lightning," the rancher's wife insisted, clucking her tongue and shaking her head in disapproval. Then, touching my arm for emphasis, she said in a conspiratorial tone, "I heard he *killed* a man."

"Shot a tin cup out of a man's hand at more 'n a hundred yards—in the dark—with no scope on his rifle!" an old-timer who had known John for many years confirmed. " 'Course the guy was thievin' John's trapline," the man snickered behind his whiskers just loud enough for me to hear. "Johnny figgered the scoundrel got what he deserved! Said the guy left enough furs, food, and tack to mor'n pay fer damages!"

The controversial mystique about this man inflamed my curiosity. I would not be completely at peace until I had met John Terry face to face. Call it destiny; all I knew was that I had to meet him. We lived less than 80 miles from him, but it turned out to be a challenging two and a half-hour trek over a mountain pass on unimproved logging roads that would have been impossible to navigate without our trusty old four-wheel-drive pick-up. At the end of our rut-and-bumps journey, there stood a smiling, gentle farmer, with his well-trained team of matched black Percheron horses, Dan and Pride, hitched to a wagonload of fresh hay. We helped him with his haying for awhile, and then we invited him to join us as we spread our picnic lunch beneath the tall spruce trees at the edge of his "Black Forest."

Before the day was over John had identified us from a dream he'd had seventeen years earlier. It *was* destiny! He looked at Jere and said, "My Guide *told* me that you would *teach* me how to *pray*, Jere, that you had *answers* to my questions. I've asked every pastor I know about the strange question my angel guide said that you would know the answer to..." Jere was only too happy to study the Bible with him; John asked questions, Jere gave him answers. Before long, John had quit smoking, and mostly quit swearing, and had asked Jere to help him become a Christian. Their bond was enviable; they were brothers in faith, and they were both Irish.

In spite of the fact that John's ranch was far off the beaten track, the roughhewn timbers leading to his cabin door were well-worn with traffic from many walks of life; most notably traceable among them were the impressions left by numerous, long-time friends. There were boot prints

1977 Photo of Jere Franklin and John Terry

belonging to RCMP officers who, more often than not, were seeking John's advice. The occasional television crew dropped in by helicopter and traipsed into his cabin to record John's commentary on political issues, for he was a well-informed citizen. There were the superficial impressions of more than one renowned politician seeking John's sanction. There were even the frenzied tracks of hapless victims who wandered into John's life with real need, and the evidence was clear that more than one life was saved by John's quick thinking and common sense. There was, of course, the irate stomping of a few sworn enemies who sought John's wilderness cabin to purposely reignite the torch they carried against him. Friend or foe, John never turned anyone away. He generally offered every visitor a mug of tea from the kettle simmering at the back of his ancient wood cook stove.

I can't count how many times I left my own prints on the walkway to John's cabin. During our son's growing up years, we made a practice of visiting his "Uncle John" at least once a year to celebrate their birthdays in the month of May, always enjoying a fragrant cup of the wild mint from the luxuriant growth that bordered his beloved Wolverine River.

With the progression of years we noted, with deep regret, that The Wolverine Valley was changing. The very horizon line was being eroded by industry; Beautiful Quintette Mountain, framed by Uncle John's kitchen window was being carved away, layer by layer, for coal export. He was nearly killed and left with permanent scarring when his horses stampeded because of the severe impact of the blast before it was properly regulated. In order to transport the coal, a railroad track passed within meters of his cabin door, then continued on through the bush to dissect his precious beaver pond before tunneling through the Rocky Mountains to Prince George. Eight of his friendly pack horses were killed on the tracks, and the noise of the train prevented his beloved geese from nesting on the abandoned beaver pond.

Try as he might to prevent encroachment, it was painfully evident that Uncle John was losing the battle to protect his sanctuary. Bird songs were muffled by the snarl of chain saws cutting right-of-ways on nearby slopes. Wildlife did not react favorably to the seismic explosions mandatory to oil and gas exploration. With each of our successive visits to the J bar W, it became more challenging to discern the pristine beauty that had drawn Uncle John to this secluded valley back in the late 1940s. After being wounded in WWII, his body and soul were in disrepair. Full of hate, disillusioned with life in general, he traveled west and set up a shoe repair business in Dawson Creek, British Columbia where he ran smack into Kate Edwards somewhere around 1948. Fortunately, Old Aunt Kate, didn't judge him for his incurable restlessness and socially unacceptable outbursts. In spite of the age gap, they were kindred spirits. Having had the same kind of trouble at just about his age, Kate told him some of her story, and that she might have the solution to his dilemma.

"Come on over when you've finished sewing boots today and I'll show you something, Johnnie. It's something I've been saving for someone special. I'm pretty sure that someone is you!" And that night, when Kate answered his knock, her wise old eyes sparkled with a light that folks in Dawson Creek seldom saw except when she'd safely delivered another baby in the Peace Country.

"Johnnie, it was back in 1911 that I discovered an enchanting stream in a hidden valley about three hard days' ride from here. That stream helped heal my pain. It'll help you, too, if you listen carefully to the secrets of the Wolverine." Though John was slightly intoxicated, the disillusioned cowboy focused with interest on Aunt Kate's "secret"—a map of her beloved homestead in the Wolverine Valley. When he sobered up, it didn't take John long to direct his energies toward escaping from civilization; within weeks he'd sold his shoe repair business, given Aunt Kate what she was asking for her homestead, bought three horses, and headed southwest, into the Rocky Mountains.

He found the healing stream; he drank from it, fished from it, watered his garden with it, and even swam in it on hot days. Most often, though, at the end of the day, he would just watch the sunset and listen to the soft murmurings of the picturesque stream.

In 1974, the same spirit of adventure that called John Terry to the Wolverine Valley also beckoned Jere to Canada's Peace Country. Though we also lived without electricity, visiting the J bar W was like traveling back in time at least a hundred years—like a pioneer village come to life—the setting unmarred with man-made devices, the friendly horses, the beaver pond, the geese, the pile of firs ready for shipping, the ancient cook stove with its simmering teakettle—all were utilitarian and artistic at the same time—the country look. Uncle John was happy to do without electricity in order to protect his sanctuary. His cabin and its surroundings were a heritage for which he was willing to do most anything to protect. There was no obligation to fill the quiet spaces of our visits with small talk; indeed, moments of pure silence became ever more valuable with the encroachment of industrialization.

His tea-kettle matched his temper—always hot! But he was just as ready to bless the good as to battle the evil. Heated discussions, like honey in his tea, were most often sweetened with comedy. In the early days of our acquaintance he was openly amused at my gullibility to be entangled in his blarney. I never recognized that he was feeding me a yarn until his chuckle and grin affirmed my ignorance.

On May 8, Uncle John's birthday, we generally brought him a flower basket from our greenhouse. He always saved one hook to hang his basket from, but by early May, his feeders were filled and hung awaiting the arrival of the migratory hummingbirds. Knowing my love of birds, he pointed out a particularly rambunctious male that appeared to be slightly larger than the other hummers, and who chattered in a most commanding manner, boldly laying claim to every drop of nectar in the territory, including the petunias in the hanging basket. The other hummers backed away whenever he approached their food source. The noisy hum of his wings seemed much louder than any of the hummingbirds at our own cabin. I associated the sound of his wings with the metallic rattling of the motor on the old VW bug we had during my growing up years back in Portland, Oregon.

"Hear that, Linda?" Uncle John asked, indicating the rambunctious Rufous. "That one's Big Motor. He's been comin' t' m' feeder fer at least six years, now. First one back ever' spring. If I don't have the feeders up, he peeks through m' kitchen window t' remind me. If I happen t' have the door open, he comes right on inta m' cabin!" he chuckled to himself and added, "Most welcome, too! Good comp'ny. Better'n most, actually! If the bird book didn't say otherwise, I'd've have guessed he drifted over here on a roving Irish wind! Creates a reg'lar donnybrook wherever he goes! An' he's so *full* o' the blarney!"

"He razzes me, Linda," Uncle John continued in a more serious tone. "When I tell 'im not t'be so angry and bossy with his friends, he looks me right in the eye 'n' says, 'Look whose talkin', Mad Trapper! You cuss at the railroad engineers every time the train comes through!'"

19

Uncle John's years in the wilderness had helped him deal with life's injustices; he sometimes told me of the spiritual lessons he'd been gleaning from his garden, the animals, and the flowers.

Time, and his river, somewhat subdued Uncle John's rage, but he remained annoyed with the hand that life had dealt him and blamed the leftover irritations on the threats of modernization and his Irish ancestry. It was the genetic justifications that had dubbed him, "The Mad Trapper."

When we came out to the J bar W on his 88th birthday, Uncle John was walking with a cane. He was down to one dog and there seemed to be fewer horses, too. There was still snow on Quintette, but it was mostly black. After filling three mugs for us, he sat back down in his favorite wooden chair with a heavy sigh.

"It's only wilderness once," he said, stirring a generous spoonful of sugar into his tea. "How can the destruction of God's beautiful earth be classified as progress?"

Looking toward the barn I could clearly see that the garden was not planted, in fact, it wasn't even cultivated. Focusing closer, I was glad to see that he had hung his hummingbird feeders.

"Uncle John, I see that you are feeding your hummingbirds," I said, "but you aren't planting a garden this year?"

"Big Motor didn't come back," he said, staring vacantly into his steaming cup. "Just didn't feel right to plant it without him." I hadn't realized how much he counted on the saucy mini-angel's blessing. Though he seemed hopeful of seeing Big Motor once more, I realized, with a sting in my heart, that Uncle John would never plant another garden. Jere and our son, Jed, excused themselves to take their annual walk through the Green Chapel. Uncle John and I finished our tea in comfortable silence my mind considering how he was going to adjust to this aging process.

How long will Uncle John be able to stay in his cabin alone? It will be more and more difficult for him to bring in his wood to keep his fire burning.

Good thing it's the spring of the year...if only I had a story to read to him... or maybe brought my accordion to play some hymns for him. I don't have a good feeling about his deteriorating condition...

When Jere and Jed returned from the Green Chapel Jere read to Uncle John about the new earth from the well-worn Bible on his kitchen table, and then we had prayer with him. He seemed to take up less space in the doorway of his cabin as he waved goodbye to us with his cane.

A few weeks later, rumors began circulating in our little hometown of Chetwynd that our beloved Uncle John was not expected to live through the summer. Though Jere had always been concerned that we not "wear out our welcome at the J bar W," this time we didn't delay. When we saw Uncle John, his pain was evident; the twinkle in his eye was gone, the tea-kettle cold. Jere, read from Uncle John's well-worn Bible and prayed with him, as usual, and then he and Jed walked toward the river by way of the Green Chapel. I stayed behind to play a song or two for Uncle John, and just as I pulled my accordion out of its case, I heard a train whistle in the distance.

Hoping to camouflage the unwelcome interruption of Sabbath peace, I quickly began playing *Life is Like a Mountain Railroad*. Uncle John grinned, tapping the edge of his old wooden table with a spoon in time to the music. Not knowing how long we might be able to hear the train whistle, I ran a collection of his favorites together, hymns like: *The Old Rugged Cross, There's a Family Bible On the Table, I'll Fly Away,* and *Rock of Ages*. When I stopped, the train was gone. I leaned on my accordion while we shared a companionable silence that he quietly interrupted.

"They want to take me to a nursing home, Linda," Uncle John frowned. "Y'know I can't go, don't cha? My home's here...in the wilderness...what's left of it. This is where I learned to really live, and it's where I choose to die. Remember my poem?" He repeated for me, from memory, the mean-ingful words that had come to him some forty years before.

The Lure of the Wild

There's a six-point buck a-swinging
Near my cabin on the hill
Though the wolves have oft pursued him
He's escaped their lust to kill.

Watching o'er his mate and offspring
This old monarch of the glen
Used to match his native cunning
'Gainst the wiles of skillful men.

As I sit upon my doorstep
Gazing on the purple haze,
Then my mind is prone to wander
Thinking of those happy days.

Just to watch the timid beaver
When he thinks I'm nowhere near
Is a thrill to make the conquest
Equal to the hunt for deer.

In the night the mournful screech owl
Wakes the echoes with his cry,
While the dumb, nearsighted porky
Chews the timbers where I lie.

When the lake's unrippled surface
Is disturbed by feeding trout,
All the black flies in the country
Couldn't stop me going out.

For the urge is strong within me
To beat nature at her game
Stronger than the quest for riches,
Worldly wealth, or fleeting fame.

Not for me those human anthills
With the traffic's roar and squeal.
Not for me those man-made prisons
Made of mortar, brick, and steel.

For my little cabin calls me
Far from noises rude and harsh;
Where in spring the chesty bullfrog
Sends his call across the marsh.

And when I'm old and weary
And my time on earth is still
Let my bones rest here in freedom
By my cabin on the hill.

As he finished the poem, he winced and began rubbing his neck. I set my accordion aside and tenderly applied a mixture of essential oils that I felt might help relieve his pain.

"Thanks, Linda," he nodded slowly. "That does ease the pain. Gets bad, sometimes." I left the little bottle of oil on his windowsill hoping he would use it while he watched his beloved hummers. I was glad to see that the feeders still held nectar. I played one last hymn, *Lord Give Me a Cabin in the Corner of Gloryland*.

"Yep, Linda, that's all I want—a little cabin over yonder," he said as I finished the song. Motioning out the window toward the cloudless July sky he declared with a speck of his old spunk, "As for me, I'll rent out my mansion to the city folks!"

Silence reigned as we looked toward the Green Chapel where Jere and Jed were sitting together on a rough-hewn bench in Uncle John's outdoor church. Everyone was welcomed there, especially the squirrels who made their homes in the towering spruce trees above the slowly meandering Wolverine River. Uncle John's finishing touch was to create a "forest pulpit". He chose a huge spruce burl; cutting it diagonally, he left a four foot length of trunk attached to form the pedestal. Simply elegant. In Uncle John's Chapel, there was seating for a hundred people—or just one. It was always open—the same way Uncle John pictured God—with arms widespread and full of pardoning secrets.

"I've had a good life, Linda," he smiled. "I try t' live by the conclusions I've reached, quietly sitting out there in my Green Chapel talkin' t' God… some folks think they can ignore Him six days of the week and that He'll be there when they come t' Him on the seventh," Uncle John observed as we watched Jed coax a squirrel toward his outstretched hand. "It just isn't so. Ya gotta live *every day* with Him. Ya gotta *respect* God *and* yer fella man. *Then*, when ya come to Him on the seventh day, He'll *listen* t' ya! Ya can't just polish your shoes and go to church. Yer *heart* needs polished, too. Ever' day."

The loving God of the great outdoors had become real to Uncle John. This was the God who had helped him begin to learn patience from a hummingbird—when he chose to listen. This same God quietly stood aside and watched Uncle John let his Irish temper make a bad situation worse when he chose not to listen.

This same God miraculously arranged for Jed and me to be at Uncle John's side during the closing moments of his life. On August 5, 2000, we just "happened" to be in the town of Tumbler Ridge, and just "happened" to step into the clinic for the first time in our lives, and there was Uncle John's son, James in the waiting room. I was surprised to see him there and asked how his father was doing.

"Not so good, Linda. He's here in ER right now," James explained. "We brought him in not long ago." He went on to say that he and his friend had been staying out at the J bar W to help his father for the past few weeks. That morning he had suffered what Dr. Helm thought was quite possibly a massive stroke. My lab tech background put me at ease with hospital protocol, and Dr. Helm and I knew each other from community awareness projects. Dr. Helm had been Uncle John's physician for more than ten years and I knew that he was aware of our connection, so, although Jed and I were not technically classified as "family," I didn't hesitate to approach him for permission.

"You can see him until the ambulance is ready, Linda," said Dr. Helm. "We are preparing to transport him to the Dawson Creek hospital shortly."

Thank you, Lord for these precious moments. Your timing is incredible. Help me know what to say to Uncle John.

Though he seemed agitated, his hands and arms restless, his eyes were closed and it was unlikely he knew anything about his surroundings. I took his right hand and leaned down close to his ear

"Hi Uncle John," I spoke quietly. "Jed and I are here with you." His wild thrashing relaxed a little. Uncle John had taught me that it wasn't necessary to fill all the moments with small talk, but if this was goodbye I needed closure. I prayed for the right words.

"You rest, now, Uncle John. God be with you." When the ambulance attendants came in, it was with heavy hearts that Jed and I watched Uncle John disappear. Within just a few short hours, he fell into his long sleep.

Uncle John's daughter, Mary Anne, asked Jere to officiate her father's memorial service. On May 13 the train was respectfully quiet as family and friends gathered in the Green Chapel where Uncle John's cowboy hat hung on the back of his empty kitchen chair. Friends and family testified, with tears and laughter, about their views of John Wesley Terry; soldier, cowboy, trapper, woodsman, philosopher, and father.

When Uncle John's daughter, Mary Anne, asked our family to participate in sprinkling Uncle John's ashes over the land he loved, the Wolverine River beckoned me. I walked upstream to a deep pool not far from where Aunt Kate's cabin had stood—Uncle John's first sanctuary—where his restless soul had learned to listen. I pictured Uncle John the last day we had seen him, leaning on his mossy old garden fence, one hand gripping the walking stick he had carved from a diamond willow. He looked so tired, as if he had earned his rest. I held that picture in my mind's eye as I trickled my handful of ashes into the clear, green water. Sunlight reflected the glistening whiteness as the ashes settled to the bottom of the stream. I closed my eyes, finally allowing an escape for my tears. How fitting that he would rest here, just as he had wished in his poem, how did he put it? "...by my cabin on the hill."

I can't even guess how long I stood there on the riverbank, but as I wiped my eyes and looked at the ground beneath my feet, a clover plant gradually came into focus. In the midst of it, there was a perfect four-leaf clover smiling back at me! I was reminded of Uncle John's Irish ancestry, his heritage link with Jere, his love of blarney, his hot temper, and how he credited Big Motor with the cooling of it. I recalled some of his object lessons from flowers, his courage in the face of danger, the pain he bravely suffered during his last days, and the incredible coincidence that allowed me to be the last person to whisper a final prayer to him.

Clutching my little green Irish blessing, I walked slowly back to Uncle John's cabin. Just outside the door, I glanced up. Several hummingbirds seemed to be paying their last respects, too. One particularly saucy male Rufous darted in front of me, and hung in the air making figure eights with his tail. I knew this to be a territorial stance among our own little flock of hummingbirds back home. I stood back and let my mind wander as he drank his fill.

How many times had Uncle John filled this feeder...a hundred times... more...a thousand times at least! How many times had he anticipated the return of the hummers? Was it just a coincidence that Big Motor's fury gave him the desire to be rid of his temper? I wondered at the winds of destiny; the trapper, the hummingbird, my family, and me—such a richly designed tapestry!

Curious about how a hummingbird viewed life, I stood on tiptoe to focus through the nectar. Images were puzzling, like grotesque reflections in a carnival mirror. Objects were small, inverted, and stretched out of shape according to the contour of the container, but I was able to discern the barn, the rustic fence, the wooden hay wagon, the tall spruce trees of the Black Forest, cars, pick-ups, and eventually able to even recognize individual guests. The sky looked so big compared to the rest of the picture—maybe even big enough to hold my sorrow until, somewhere beyond the blue, my tears would be forever wiped away. Uncle John would want me to understand the sweetness in the lesson of loss.

Now we see only puzzling reflections in a mirror,
but then we shall see face to face.

Sometimes life is puzzling; at other times the lessons come so clear. What makes the difference? Can "bad" circumstances teach us "good" lessons? With a little celestial coaching, the inner ear is able to discern healing messages. Old Aunt Kate had that kind of insight, and, thankfully, young Johnnie took her advice. In the restorative atmosphere of the Wolverine Valley, Uncle John quietly contemplated the ways of the wilderness, and gradually accepted the soothing touch of his Creator. He was enabled to discern personal messages in the object lessons of nature. That's how he discerned the extraordinary message delivered by his little friend, a tiny angel with the very unlikely name of Big Motor. And listening made all the difference.

A Song from Sylvan

The little cares that fretted me,
I lost them yesterday
Among the fields above the sea,
Among the winds at play;
Among the lowing herds,
The rustling of the trees,
Among the singing birds,
The humming of the bees.

The fears of what may come to pass,
I cast them all away,
Among the clover-scented grass,
Among the new-mown hay;
Among the husking of the corn,
Where drowsy poppies nod,
Where ill thoughts die and good are born,
Out in the fields with God.

—*Louise Imogene Guiney*

The Soldier and the Hen

Roy F. Cottrell

*"... your Father knoweth what things ye have
need of before ye ask him."*

—Matthew 6:8

*A*n injured soldier lay dying on the battlefield, out of reach of
the medics in the thick of the battle. Help came to him in a
most remarkable way; not once, but five times, lest he be left
with any doubt as to the source of his relief. For each of us, there are times in
life when extremity is our only option. How else can we begin to understand
that God is an opportunist anxiously waiting to inscribe upon every human
heart a special message of His unconditional love?

Before enlisting, Thomas had been greatly impressed by the lectures
of an evangelist on the second coming of Christ, but later cast aside all
thought of religion. In 1916, in the Battle of the Somme, he was hit by
a piece of shrapnel and fell helpless and bleeding in a hollow place on
the field. The continued deadly hum of bullets prevented the ambulance
corps from coming to the rescue of the wounded.

The next morning as the soldier was giving himself up to die, a hen
came out from a nearby farmhouse and laid an egg at his side. Thomas

ate it and was strengthened. On the four succeeding mornings the faithful hen came with her life-sustaining gift. When the storm of battle passed, the soldier was rescued. Upon his hospital bed he thanked God for his remarkable deliverance. When Thomas was at last able to return to his home, he became a door-to-door seller of Christian books.

Thomas was forever grateful to that little hen for saving his life. But she did not just save his life; she recruited him into the greatest of all "armed forces"! Who would have ever thought that a friendly little hen could win a toughened, battle-weary soldier to the Lord's army?

Like the widow with the two mites who gave all she had, that little hen gave what she could and the Lord used it to save a life, for eternity!

(*Signs of the Times*, June 13, 1939)

A Strange Singer

Joy's the shyest bird
Mortal ever heard;
Listen rapt and silent while he sings;
Do not seek to see,
Lest the vision be
But a flutter of departing wings.

Straight down out of heaven
Drops the fiery leaven,
Beating, burning, rising in his breast;
Never, never long
Canst thou bear the song,
All too high for labour or for rest?

Hope can sit and sing
With a folded wing,
Long contented in a narrow cage;
Patience on the nest,
Hour by hour will rest,
Brooding tender things in hermitage.

Singers true and sweet,
Mockers bright and fleet,
Close about thy door they flit and call;
One that will not stay
Draws thy heart away;
Listen! listen! It is more than all.

—*Caroline Spencer*

Set Free

"He hath sent me to bind up the brokenhearted,
to proclaim liberty to the captives,
and the opening of the prison to them that are bound."

—Isaiah 61:1

George Thomas was a pastor in a small New England town. One Easter Sunday he came to the church carrying a rusty, bent, old bird cage, and set it by the pulpit. Eyebrows were raised and, as if in response, Pastor Thomas began to speak.

"I was walking through town yesterday when I saw a young boy coming toward me swinging this bird cage. On the bottom of the cage were three little wild birds, shivering with cold and fright. I stopped the lad.

"What do you have there, son?"

"Just some old birds," came the reply.

"What are you going to do with them?" I asked.

"Take 'em home and have fun with 'em," he answered. "I'm gonna tease 'em and pull out their feathers to make 'em fight. I'm gonna have a real good time."

"But you'll get tired of those birds sooner or later. What will you do then?"

"Oh, I got some cats," said the little boy. "They like birds. I'll take 'em to them."

The pastor was silent for a moment. "How much do you want for those birds, son?"

"Huh? Why, you don't want them birds, mister. They're just plain old field birds. They don't sing. They ain't even pretty!"

"How much?" the pastor asked again.

The boy sized up the pastor as if he were crazy and said, "Ten dollars?"

The pastor reached into his pocket and took out a ten dollar bill. He placed it in the boy's hand. In a flash, the boy was gone. The pastor picked up the cage and gently carried it to the end of the alley where there was a tree and a grassy spot. Setting the cage down, he opened the door, and by softly tapping the bars persuaded the birds to fly out, setting them free.

Well, that explained the empty bird cage on the pulpit, but the pastor continued:

One day Satan and Jesus were having a conversation. Satan had just come from the Garden of Eden, and he was gloating.

"Yes, sir, I just caught a world full of people down there. I set me a trap, used bait I knew they couldn't resist. Got 'em all!"

"What are you going to do with them?" Jesus asked.

Satan replied, "Oh, I'm gonna have fun! I'm gonna teach them how to marry and divorce each other, how to hate and abuse each other, how to drink and smoke and curse. I'm gonna teach them how to invent guns and bombs and kill each other. I'm really gonna have fun!"

"And what will you do when you are done with them?" Jesus asked.

"Oh, I'll kill 'em," Satan proudly glared.

"How much do you want for them?" Jesus asked.

"Oh, you don't want those people! They ain't no good. Why, you'd love them and they'd just hate you. They'd spit on you, curse you and kill you. No, you don't want those people!"

"How much?" He asked again.

Satan looked at Jesus and sneered, "All your blood, tears, and your life."

"DONE!" Jesus said.

"Then He paid the price," said the pastor, and, picking up the cage, he walked from the pulpit.

—Anon

A Minor Bird

I have wished a bird would fly away,
And not sing by my house all day;

Have clapped my hands at him from the door
When it seemed as if I could bear no more.

The fault must partly have been in me.
The bird was not to blame for his key.

And of course there must be something wrong
In wanting to silence any song.

—*Robert Frost*

The Hunter and the Goose

Ye have condemned and killed the just;
and he doth not resist you.

—James 5:6

*W*hen my mother's good friend, Esther, told her about the Canada goose they had raised, the story that emerged was so special that I could hardly record it fast enough! Esther knew from the first day she saw the precocious little gosling that he had more than one strike against him, but of all the threats against little Gus, she was most concerned about her outspoken brother-in-law, Bob, a dyed-in-the-hide hunter. His extensive gun collection contained weapons ingeniously designed to conquer any animal that he might desire to add to his trophy collection. This is the triumphant account of a gentle crossing of two strong, very different, wills.

Jerry Corcoran had seen enough bloodshed that he vowed to raise his family in as peaceful a place as his GI grant would allow. In 1942, at age 15, he had escaped from the strictness of his parental home and was hurled headlong into WWII. After surviving his assignment in the US Navy, he discovered Esther Collins who became the light of his life. When they discovered the picturesque 130 acres overlooking the little farming town of Royal City, Washington, Jerry knew he was home. Never mind that others perceived it as a desert, it was Jerry's oasis; it had a *pond!*

While Jerry established the farm, Esther worked for School District #160 as a receptionist, secretary, payroll/board clerk, doing whatever needed to be done. Three daughters were eventually added to the Corcoran home, and Esther continued to work during the hours the girls were in school. She was not someone who could sense a need without becoming involved, and she hadn't worked for the district very long before she realized the district's desperate need of an inviting place where children could feel welcomed after school. The seed of her dream took root in Jerry's heart, and soon the Corcoran's were spending most of their free time landscaping the extensive yard with simple delights such as Jerry desired as a child.

Several weeping willow trees already graced the front yard. Jerry constructed monkey bars, a swing set, and two long picnic tables that Esther covered with red-and-white checked oilcloth. Together they shaped and planted colorful flower beds. Esther painted several wrought iron benches with shiny white enamel and clustered them around a campfire circle that she outlined with large white rocks. Jerry planted more willow saplings around his prized irrigation pond and painstakingly enlarged his agricultural waterhole until it took on the character of a charming little lake.

The mud had hardly settled in the new lake before "Royal children" poured in to test the rope swing, the little canvas canoe, and the "Walking Pole," a telephone pole Jerry had suspended a foot above the water where the children played "King of the Pond." The children knew all that they needed to know about their benefactors—"Uncle Jerry and Aunt Esther" were the perfect team for fostering happy childhood memories; they loved to laugh, and they loved children. The children affectionately dubbed their new playground Corcoran's Pond.

When their girls, Tanya, Marliss, and Muriel had a special party coming up, they would beg Jerry to pump more water in the pond. Only when they were older did they realize how much it cost their father to pipe that extra water up from Grand Coulee Dam. Though he knew much of this extra water was wasted through evaporation, there was nothing Jerry loved more than receiving a hug from one of his precious girls about him being "the best Dad in the whole wide world." Slowly, he was beginning to sense that the crop of Royal children growing up like the cattails around his little lake were of greater value than any other crop he was cultivating on his acreage.

Jerry laughingly dismissed Esther's concern about water safety, insisting that he just wanted everyone to have fun. He wouldn't even acknowledge the potential for disaster. Instead of sharing her reservations, he added a diving board at the deep end of the pond! During the most active hours, Esther policed the grounds as inconspicuously as she could—like a mother hen protecting her chicks, making sure no harm came to any stragglers, especially those children whose parents had left them without supervision. Esther inquired about the possibility of a Red Cross instructor and soon Royal children were collecting colorful swim patches that they proudly displayed on their swimsuits. Some eventually achieved lifeguard status. When the older, more experienced swimmers assigned themselves to watch over the younger children, Esther breathed a little easier.

Arrival of a Newborn

Although they had plenty of friends at school and at home, the Corcoran girls joyfully anticipated the less frequent visits of one special family who lived over in Quincy: Carl and Audrey Miksch and their two sons, Dean and Melvin. When the Miksch's arrived one sunny afternoon in the spring of 1959 with a parcel, the girls gathered around for the unveiling of their new surprise. They squealed with delight as Carl lifted the lid from the box and released a tiny gray gosling onto the driveway.

"Found him just wandering around in the woods yesterday," he explained. "Boy, was he making a racket! I couldn't see or hear any adults, and I knew Little Gus here would probably be somebody's supper before nightfall, so I stuffed him into my shirt. I figured any Canada goose'd be safe at the Royal Slope Ranch."

Esther smiled and sighed. She was amused by the precocious little bird, but her schedule hardly allowed time to care for a helpless chick. She need not have worried about Little Gus, however, for even at less than a week old he could fend for himself. He was already selectively independent, friendly, and quite opinionated. He bypassed many offers of help from human hands that first day, choosing rather to adopt the Corcoran family's friendly Weimeraner, Rogue, as his surrogate mother.

Gray Ghost

Nicknamed "The Gray Ghost," Rogue beamed with pride whenever Gus snuggled up to him. Wherever Rogue went, Gus waddled closely behind; Gus drank from Rogue's water bucket, ate his meals of cracked corn from a little dish Esther placed beside the dog's dish, and cuddled next to the dog when it was time for a nap. As the days passed, gosling-sitting became less enchanting to Rogue. Baby Gus demanded constant companionship, so, unless someone "borrowed" Gus for awhile to give Rogue a break, the dog often demonstrated signs of emotional suffocation by early afternoon. His energetic new friend insisted on a full day's worth of action. He even interrupted Rogue's usual nap-time by nibbling on the dog's velvety ears just as he was entering Doggie Dreamland where there were no exhausting little goslings to care for. It took him a few days, but Rogue ingeniously solved his problem; he put Gus to bed for a nap.

When Rogue needed a break he would walk toward the edge of the pond and plop down in the shade of a certain willow, convincingly feigning exhaustion right beside the nest that Jerry had built for Gus at the edge of the pond. Baby Gus would tip his head from side to side, look down at the inert hound and begin gently pecking at him to remind the gray ghost of his fatherly duties. If that invoked no response, Gus would begin pulling on the dog's ears, his tail, his toes, and toenails. Exercising utmost discipline, Rogue kept his body limp and his eyes squeezed tightly shut, no doubt envisioning the freedom he would enjoy if he could only tolerate the torture without reacting.

Discouraged by the dog's lack of response, Gus would finally waddle away and "accidentally" discover his nest. Except for the eye that followed Gus until he finally climbed into his nest, Rogue remained totally inert as the gosling tucked his head under a wing, and fell asleep. The instant Rogue suspected that baby Gus was really asleep, he would rise and quietly sneak to the edge of the pond, and then very slowly turn his head sideways just far enough to see if any little black webbed feet were padding across the grass behind him. If his escape was successful, Rogue would bound away like the wind, clownishly romping through the alfalfa fields, whirling in circles of ecstasy, trying not to bark lest his freedom be cut short. Then he might take a nap, or just amble around the acreage—blissfully alone. After a stretch of much-deserved privacy, Rogue would wander back toward the nest and lay down beside his friend, ready to resume his fatherly duties when Gus awakened.

Gus Island

Like the children in the community, Gus also learned to swim in Corcoran's Pond. When he was still very young, Esther and the three girls gave their gosling a swimming lesson. The four of them piled into their little rowboat while Baby Gus, in the agony of abandonment, finally splashed into the water and began comically paddling along behind them. It didn't take long for Gus to find his sea legs, and swimming gave him his first real taste of independence. Rogue, though he loved the water, did not follow Gus into the pond for he was more than ready for Gus to earn his independence.

Gus would swim with his own family, he even allowed a few visitors, but when the pond became too crowded, he would swim to the deep end, climb onto the diving board and squat down to supervise the activities, that is, until someone wanted to use the diving board. Then he would march to the end of the board, calculate the distance to the surface of the water, dive off and quietly paddle to his hideaway, to the one place that no human, dog, or cat would follow, Gus Island.

Every winter, when the pond was dry, Jerry would bulldoze the sediment off of the bottom of the pond in order to maintain its depth. With that sediment, and the aid of some lumber, Jerry had built the island. It was enticing to the children, perhaps simply because it was off limits, but it was the one place Jerry asked the children not to play because it could easily disappear if it was overused. Gus claimed ownership of the island; an idyllic life for any goose, until the day he realized that he had work to do.

Wonders of Flight

By the time he was a full grown gander, but before his adult plumage was complete, Gus discovered his lifelong passion—setting irrigation pipes with Farmer Jerry. By the time he received his calling, Gus appeared to be capable of flight, but was content to waddle behind his new best friend. Assuming the highest duty of friendship, Jerry urged his little buddy heavenward any way he could, hoping to fuel the desire for flight. Assuming the role of Father Goose, Jerry first trotted slowly downhill. Unable to waddle fast enough, but not wanting to lose Jerry, Gus would use his wings, like the spokes of a windmill, to propel himself forward, but he did not fly. He would stop and honk noisily until Jerry returned to calm his fears.

Unable to entice Gus into the air by running ahead of him, Jerry put the goose in the bed of his old red pickup, drove a short distance from home, removed Gus from the bed, climbed back in the truck, and took off down the field, keeping his eye on the rearview mirror. Gus panicked. He waddle-flopped as fast as he could, but he finally gave up the chase. Standing in the middle of the dirt lane, neck outstretched, he again honked loudly for the return of his beloved flight instructor.

Jerry backed up, got out and hugged the big bird, then hoisted him into the bed of the truck. Gus enjoyed riding lessons much more than flying lessons, but at least once a day, Jerry encouraged Gus to fly by purposely leaving him behind. When he pulled away, the gangly gander would waddle a short distance, then stand still—neck outstretched and wings flapping—and honk for Jerry to return. Jerry would shake his head and smile, grind the old truck into reverse, scoop up the big bird, cuddle him and, once again, toss him into the bed of the truck

One day, while Jerry was changing a pipe some distance from home during the daily flight exercise, Gus jumped out of the truck to catch a grasshopper, as usual. Intent on changing the pipes before supper, Jerry did not notice that his friend was not in the bed of the truck. When he was halfway across the field, he glanced in his rearview mirror and noticed that the bed was empty. But wait! What was that airborne object bearing down on him? It was Gus...flying! Gus quickly closed the gap, and landed in front of the truck as if to prevent Jerry's escape. Jerry stopped and hugged the big bird a little longer this time, for that was the day he had truly earned his wings. That was also the day that Gus assumed the roll of co-pilot—flying just outside Jerry's window—keeping one eye on his hero and one on the road. He no longer panicked when Jerry took off without him; he flew alongside the old red pick-up, knowing that he would receive a word of praise and a tender pat on his head, if not a full-fledged hug at the end of the journey.

Like most discoveries, flight posed new perils. Jerry had seen enough of prisons during the war that he refused to consider confining his friend, but he was concerned for the big bird's safety when he took the old farm truck to town for supplies. Gus insisted on flying beside the driver's window. When the truck stopped, Gus would land in front of the truck in traffic just as he did in the alfalfa fields! Since the old truck couldn't hold everyone in the Corcoran family, the girls took turns riding to town with their father. The best part of the trip was arriving home to share stories about Gus' highway encounters. He had acquired the worrisome habit of waiting until the last second before swooping up and over the approaching vehicles. After their first few frights, the Corcoran girls started watching expressions of the oncoming drivers. Their fear for Gus' safety was replaced with hilarious glee.

One day, while traveling toward Othello, Jerry drew up behind a truck exactly like his own old red pick-up. Gus must have blinked, for when Jerry turned off the highway he flew up beside the driver's window of the wrong truck! When Jerry noticed that Gus had disappeared, he stopped a few yards down the side road and turned around. The driver of the other pickup, after the initial shock of seeing a full-grown Canada goose flying beside him, had pulled over to the side of the main road. As soon as the truck stopped, Gus, of course, landed in front of it and cocked his head in confusion when two strange men began sneaking toward him. The men, absorbed in their hunting expedition, did not hear Jerry pull up behind them. They had just extended their arms to catch this big, crazy goose for dinner, when Jerry darted in, scooped up the big gander, and nonchalantly plopped him into the bed of his truck. In his rearview mirror, Jerry saw the two astonished men still standing beside the road, doors and mouths agape. The girls told that story for weeks, amid peals of near-breathless laughter and then praise that they had "the best goose in the whole wide world!"

Gus Games

With the approach of fall, Gus became excited about the flocks of wild geese overhead. He called to them and strained upward gaining altitudes he had never before achieved, but was not quite strong enough to join the refugees on their way to their southern paradise. To save face, Gus would end up making graceful circles around the Royal Slopes, honking excitedly, and then he'd sail back down to his pond, landing in a majestic sweep of silver spray. Watching the sky until the flock disappeared, he would, in the end, either swim out to Gus Island or make his way back to his family, demand hugs and corn, and then, more often than not, pester them for a game.

If a gentle nip did not invoke the proper attention, Gus would "play" a little harder. Because of the element of surprise, one's first experience with a "Gus Game" seemed painful, but after the Corcoran family members knew what to expect, they did not find his games too uncomfortable to endure. Some days, when the pond was not too crowded, Gus would dive underwater and nibble the Corcoran girls' toes, then surface in time to add his enthusiastic honks to their laughter.

After a hot day in the field, Jerry would sometimes lie down at the edge of his pond on the cool grass under a willow tree to relax before supper. Gus would honk with delight, quickly waddle over to Jerry, and begin nibbling the tired farmer's ears or tugging on his fingers and toes.

Of all the Gus Games, "Cat Nip" was by far the most amusing to watch. Gus never attempted to play with the cats until after he learned to fly, apparently recognizing the need of a speedy escape. He would wait until a cat was asleep, preferably with tail extended. Then, with his head snaking just above the grass, Gus would slowly creep toward the cat, his eyes alert to any sign of consciousness. If the cat roused, Gus would come to a complete halt. Arriving as close as he dared, Gus would extend his neck full length, and nip the cat's tail. The cat would leap straight up in the air, howling, hissing, and clawing. Gus would beat a hasty retreat, emitting short little grunts—his goose chuckle. If the cat attempted pursuit, Gus would rise regally into the air, glide across the yard and land on the pond, knowing that the cats would not swim after him.

If he had been more than mischievous, he could have done serious damage to the farm cats for he outweighed them, but he was a friendly goose—unpredictable and unique, to be sure, but never violent. He took no prisoners, and, as far as he knew, made no enemies. There was only one person that he could have considered a foe, but there was just no room for fear in his trusting heart.

Hunter Bob

Bob Bartges was married to Esther's sister, Edna. Although the two men were as different as night and day, Jerry and Bob were good friends.

Unlike Jerry, Bob's war experience had fueled the spirit of pursuit. The Bartges family came up from their home in Salem, Oregon to the Corcoran farm for a visit soon after Gus was adopted. Bob was taken aback when the young gander waddled up to him, looked him in the eye, tugged gently on his pant leg, and honked a friendly greeting as if to say, "You're new around here, aren't you? I don't believe I've had the pleasure of your acquaintance! Come on down here where I can get a good look at you!"

Bob immediately squatted down in front of Gus, the first wild animal he had ever encountered who refused to be afraid of him. If Gus had seen Bob's trophy collection, he might justifiably have panicked for Bob was, first and foremost, a hunter. The Bartges' roomy log home was a zoo of sorts where lifelike displays of deer, elk, moose, rabbits, squirrels, wild goats, bighorn sheep, antelope, and many species of birds were arrayed picturesquely on walls, display cases, and tables. One of Bob's greatest taxidermy masterpieces was a Canada goose caught in the act of straining toward a destination at which he would never arrive. But, there was no contest as to the winner that first day. Gus was openly affectionate, and Bob followed the gosling out to the pond for the first of many talks. Bob fed him cracked corn, and spent several hours praising and petting him. After that day, Bob always included stories of "the greatest gander in the world" in his anthology of incredible tales. And Bob was a grand story-teller—skillfully weaving humorous yarns among the threads of truth so that his listener willingly swallowed the bait before he realized that Bob had fed him a line. Like the Pied Piper, a string of youngsters usually followed Bob wherever he went, all would-be hunters jostling for position about who might go with "Uncle Bob" on his next excursion.

Bob's affiliation with Gus was even more incongruous than his relationship with his peace-loving brother-in-law. He had learned to love Jerry for his wife's sake, but Gus was another type of challenge entirely. Bob had never met a goose he wouldn't shoot, but here stood a wild bird, trustingly gazing into the eyes of his "enemy". Poor Bob! He just couldn't help subconsciously rubbing his thumb and trigger finger together when Gus grew into a magnificent gander, a perfect specimen.

Bob lived for hunting. His gun collection was his pride and joy. Dozens of rifles, pistols, shotguns, and several collectors' pieces, all in mint condition, were displayed in numerous locked cabinets throughout the house. He could quote the model number, manufacturer, manufacturing date, and every idiosyncrasy of each piece in his collection. He'd had them all apart, fine-tuned them, cleaned and shined them, and spoke of each gun as if it was a personal acquaintance. A firearm was never far from Bob's reach. But he wasn't ready to trade a gun…yet.

"Jerry, I'll trade you my car for your goose," Bob offered as that first visit came to an end. It was an enticing offer, for Jerry did admire Bob's car; it was roomy enough for him, Esther, and all three girls at once—stylish, too. Jerry just smiled, one hand caressing the friendly honker's head, the other indicating "no deal" to his incorrigible brother-in-law.

Over the next year, Bob came as often as he could, anticipating his next meeting with Gus all the way from Salem. He was never disappointed for Gus always waddled out to meet him, honking with delight, sharing secrets that only the two of them seemed to fully comprehend. To others it was a mystery, like a scene from the new earth described in Isaiah 65:25.

The wolf and the lamb shall feed together, and the lion shall eat straw like the bullock: and…they shall not hurt nor destroy in all my holy mountain, saith the LORD.

Whatever it was that the hunter and the goose discussed, Bob always came away shaking his head with greater admiration. As time passed, Bob made larger and larger offers of barter for Jerry's splendid gander, even going so far as to offer him a precious gun or two in trade.

Into the Sunset

Within a few days of Bob's last visit, Gus mysteriously disappeared. All of the Corcoran's, Rogue included, hunted for Gus in every likely and unlikely place, always watching the horizon hoping that he had just flown a little farther than usual, maybe found a playmate of his own kind, and would return before the next sunset. Jerry drove the old farm truck for miles around the neighborhood in ever-widening circles, but no goose appeared in his rear view mirror. His pickup bed, like his heart, remained empty. Esther phoned all of the neighbors, but no one had seen Gus. The Corcoran girls were devastated.

Several weeks after his disappearance, a neighbor boy, the son of a local farmer, finally confessed, giving Jerry an excuse that sounded about as hollow as a gun barrel.

"I didn't know it was *Gussy*, Mister Corcoran!" Johnnie whined, "I thought it was a *wild* goose."

Johnnie had played with Gus, and taken swimming lessons in Gus' pond, but he must not have allowed the gander to touch him in quite the same way as Gus had connected with Bob. Even during his roughest game, "Cat Nip," most folks knew that Gus never intended harm. Johnnie had not quite allowed Gus' message to cross the species barrier.

Loneliness hovered like a dark cloud over Royal Acres when his family learned the truth—Gus was never coming home again.

Final Offer

The next spring Jerry set his irrigation pipes alone. He often caught himself glancing hopefully in the rearview mirror. Then, somewhere deep down in his chest, the empty ache would rise, latch onto something in his throat and cause a tear to inch its way through the salt-and-pepper stubble on his cheek. Once again, he would swipe at the unbidden moisture with the back of his work-worn hand, shift his old truck into a higher gear, and close the nostalgic memory with a half-chuckle.

Yes, Jerry knew that his gangly chick was a heaven-directed foretaste of that new earth where there is promised to be no more tears, no more death, no cause for sorrow—and no more shooting—ever. Getting to know Gus was the only way that Hunter Bob could have ever caught the vision that inspired his final offer of trade. At the last farewell, he had looked Jerry in the eye and, with a catch in his voice, paid Jerry's gander the greatest compliment that a hunter could give a bird.

"Jerry," entreated the hunter, "I'll trade you…my whole gun collection for that goose!"

Bob White

Out near the links where I go to play
My favorite game from day to day,
There's a friend of mine that I've never met,
Walked with, or broken bread with, yet
I've talked to him oft and he's talked to me
Whenever I've been where he chanced to be;
He's a cheery old chap who keeps out of sight
A gay little fellow whose name is Bob White.

Bob White! Bob White! I can hear him call
As I follow the trail to my little ball—
Bob White! Bob White! With a note of cheer
That was just designed for a mortal ear.
Then I drift far off from the world of men
And I send an answer right back to him then;
An' we whistle away to each other there,
Glad of the life that is ours to share.

Bob White! Bob White! May you live to be
The head of a numerous family!
May you boldly call your friends out here,
With never an enemy's gun to fear.
I'm a better man as I pass along,
For your cheery call and your bit of song.
May your food be plenty and your skies be bright
To the end of your days, good friend, Bob White!

—*Edgar Guest*

The Gift of the Dove

Dr. R. T. Kendall

And Jesus, when he was baptized,
went up straightway out of the water:
and, lo, the heavens were opened unto him,
and he saw the Spirit of God
descending like a dove, and lighting upon him:
and lo a voice from heaven, saying,
"This is my beloved Son, in whom I am well pleased."

—Matthew 3:16, 17

Dr. Kendall has done much research, not only on doves and pigeons, but on the Holy Spirit as well. With his permission, the following excerpt is taken from the first chapter of his book, "The Sensitivity of the Spirit."

A few years ago a British couple, Sandy and Bernice, accepted a call from their denomination to be missionaries in Israel. A house was provided for them near Jerusalem. After they moved into their new home they noticed that a dove had come to live in the eaves of the house. They were honored to be living near Jerusalem and were particularly thrilled to have the dove come and live there. They considered it to be something of a seal of approval from the Lord, a confirmation that they were in the right place.

Sandy noticed an unsettling pattern in the dove's behavior, however. Every time a door slammed shut, or if there was a lot of noise in the house or they raised their voices, the dove would be disturbed and flutter off, and sometimes not return for a good while. This worried Sandy and he felt they were in danger of frightening the dove off permanently. With this in mind, he brought up the matter with his wife.

"Have you noticed that every time there is a lot of noise, or if we slam the door, the dove flies away?" he asked.

"Yes, and it makes me feel sad," Bernice replied. "I am afraid the dove will fly away and never come back."

"Well," said Sandy, "Either the dove will adjust his behavior to us or, if we really want to make sure we never lose him, we will have to adjust our behavior to the dove."

Watching that dove was a daily reminder to that precious couple. It changed their lives forever. There are some visible and temperamental differences between pigeons and the dove which symbolizes the Holy Spirit as it came to rest on Jesus at His baptism in the Jordan. The more I learn about the person of the Holy Spirit, and the nature of the turtle dove, the more extraordinary I find this Biblical account of the dove's blessing on Jesus. First, it is unusual—probably unprecedented—for a dove ever to alight on a human being. But for the dove to *remain* is astonishing, indeed. I don't know if our Heavenly Father chose the dove as one of the first symbols in the New Testament for the Holy Spirit because of John the Baptist's familiarity with doves, but I do know that the dove coming down and remaining on Jesus told John all he needed to know at the time; 'this is the Son of God' (John 1:34).

The dove, especially the turtle dove, is apparently a very shy, even hypersensitive bird. You can feed the pigeons in Trafalgar Square, but probably not a turtle-dove. I doubt a dove ever comes near Trafalgar Square. The Bible does not say that the Spirit came down from heaven as a pigeon. There would probably have been nothing unusual about a pigeon descending on an individual, or even remaining there.

Shortly after we moved to England in 1973, we came to feed the pigeons at Trafalgar Square. I took a photograph of our son, T. R., when he was seven, with four pigeons on each arm and one on his head! It would seem that such is out of the question when it comes to a turtle-dove. We now live in central London. Every spring we have to come up with a new method for getting rid of the pigeons which perch by our bedroom window, making guttural noises that wake us up too early in the morning. My wife, Louise, has tried opening the window, shooing them away with a mop or broom handle. But these pigeons seem impervious to any punishment we can administer to them. They are a terrible nuisance.

I decided to do some investigation on pigeons and doves. Despite what the encyclopedias say, I knew there must be *some* differences—at least in temperament—between pigeons and doves. But I did not have the evidence or experience to prove it. Moreover, I was quite certain that Sandy and Bernice would not scare a pigeon away with a slammed door or a heated argument. A pigeon—at least the pigeons of Trafalger Square—would adjust to nearly any situation, but almost certainly a turtle-dove would not.

An unexpected invitation came our way in August 1999. Our old and dear friend, Pete Cantrell from Oklahoma, whom I happened to quote in my book, *The Anointing: Yesterday, Today, Tomorrow* ("The greatest freedom is having nothing to prove!"), arranged for me to preach where he goes to church in Ada, Oklahoma. After Louise and I arrived, Pete wanted to show me his pigeons! I did not know until then that he has raised pigeons and turtledoves all his life. Pete is a Cherokee Indian and inherited a love for doves. His middle name is Grayson, after the Grayson dove.

I couldn't believe it! I told him virtually everything I have written above, and that I was confused between the supposed similarity between pigeons and doves. I have talked with some of the top experts on doves and pigeons on both sides of the Atlantic, and they all insist that there is virtually no difference between pigeons and doves—unless, however, it is the turtle-dove. There are many kinds of pigeons and many kinds of doves, but, says Pete Cantrell, the turtle-dove is different.

"First," Pete said, "I sometimes question whether they should be in the same family because of the homing instinct. A pigeon has a homing instinct—a turtle-dove has none." Pete was speaking out of fifty years of experience in raising doves and pigeons, and observing them carefully. He made the following observations:

1. Turtle doves never fight; pigeons fight with each other all the time!
2. Turtle doves can't stand noise; but pigeons don't mind.
3. Turtle doves are afraid of humans; pigeons are not.
4. Turtle doves are not defensive or territorial; but pigeons will bully for a perch.
5. Turtle doves can't be trained; but pigeons have a useable homing instinct.
6. Turtle doves won't return when released from a cage; but pigeons come back.
7. Turtle doves mate for life; but pigeons sometimes have more than one mate.

After teaching me a few differences Pete added, "A pigeon could never be the symbol of the Holy Spirit. Can you imagine a love song or a poem about the loud and boisterous pigeon?"

In his discussion of the fruit of the Spirit in Galatians 5:23, Paul includes gentleness. It is my view that the genuine presence of the Holy Spirit is not as common as we may want to believe. It is also my fear that many of us have run slipshod over this matter and have forgotten that the Holy Spirit is a very, very sensitive person. I know that I have been guilty in this area. I have joined in conversations with those who appear to feel no great anguish when speaking disparagingly of others. Real conscientiousness with regard to grieving the Spirit by attitudes and words seems absent. I would go so far as to say that it is the easiest thing in the world to grieve the Spirit. Anger, bitterness, resentment, and an unforgiving spirit come so naturally. The enemy of our soul would have us, by immorality or attitude, grieve the Spirit away. As with Ancient Israel, the enemy watches for every opportunity to chase away the Dove. The sober truth is that God will not bend the rules for any of us, regardless of our "official" position.

If we don't watch what we do and say,
The precious Dove will fly away.

Come Holy Spirit, Heavenly Dove

Come Holy Spirit, heavenly Dove,
With all Thy quickening powers;
Kindle a flame of sacred love
In these cold hearts of ours.

O raise our thoughts from things below
From vanities and toys!
Then shall we with fresh courage go
To reach eternal joys.

Awake our souls to joyful songs;
Let pure devotions rise;
Till praise employs our joyful tongues,
And doubt forever dies.

Come Holy Spirit heavenly Dove,
With all Thy quickening powers;
Come, shed abroad a Savior's love,
And that shall kindle ours.

—*Isaac Watts (1707)*

Wild Fledglings

He healeth the broken in heart and bindeth up their wounds.

—Psalm 147:3

No one seemed to want "Wild Billy", as the children at church called the uncultivated newcomer that day. His home was not the only thing that was broken. When Lara's mother and father offered their home to the lost boy, Lara secretly hoped that Billy would become her best friend. She watched carefully, praising him for any encouraging sign of progress in his attitude. When she saw how gently he handled the young red-tailed hawk, she knew that her new brother's heart was healing.

"Whoever that little boy belongs to sure has their hands full!" Daddy whispered to Mamma that first day that we saw "Wild Billy" at church. My little sister, Mandy, and I watched in awe as the little terror in ragged jeans, openly rebelled against his Aunt Connie, Mamma's good friend. We held tightly to our parents' hands, our eyes growing wider with every expletive he directed toward the woman who had temporary custody of him. When he finally jerked his hand free of Connie's grasp and ran away, Mamma and Daddy raised their eyebrows in unison, locked eyes, and nodded imperceptibly. We knew that look. Mamma and Daddy have always had a soft spot in their hearts for misfits—children and animals alike—and something in this little fireball was irresistible.

When Connie learned that her sister was about to release Billy to Children's Services, she offered her own home to her nephew, but that turned out to be an impractical alternative. The two women loved Billy, but readily admitted that he was completely out of control. Even as an eight-year-old he was involved in a street gang and had developed ferocious habits. During the time that Billy stayed with Connie, he not only destroyed her personal property, threw rocks at moving cars, and bullied younger children, but he also instigated an undercurrent of rebellion that surfaced among the young people at church.

Love and Discipline

Billy needed discipline, but my parents knew that he needed love, too. Whenever we met together in our family circle over the next few weeks, one, or each of us, would mention his name in prayer. When Billy's mother learned that Mamma and Daddy would take him, she gladly signed him into my parents' custody.

Our adopted brother, Terry, was just Mandy's age, and the two of them had already formed a close bond. Billy was the same age as me, and I coveted his friendship. However, I was more than a little concerned about his raw edges.

After he came to live with us, we noticed slight improvements in Billy's attitude, but he was still a rebel at heart. He didn't like having to obey, he didn't like keeping a schedule, and he absolutely hated eggs! When Mamma cooked eggs for breakfast, he refused to eat even one bite. Mysteriously, our hens began disappearing, one at a time, until we had no more hens to lay those problematic eggs. It wasn't until a couple of months after Billy was with us that he gave Mamma a clue as to why he hated eggs so much. We were shopping for rubber boots for him when he exploded, "I hate those boots! They're just like the ones my Daddy's girlfriend used to beat me with if I didn't eat all of the eggs she cooked!"

Billy did not respond favorably to ordinary forms of discipline and often acted out his hostilities in unacceptable ways long past our bedtime.

57

If he refused to settle down, Mamma would take him firmly by the hand and say, "Billy, let's go for a walk." The two of them would go out into the warm Florida darkness and return long after I was asleep. They would walk for miles, Mamma firmly clutching Billy's hand, telling him whatever came into her mind about the beauties of the night and the great Creator God who had made them. Mamma's commitment to consistency never wavered, but she sure did get lots of exercise that summer! I thought Mamma might be making headway when I saw them returning near dawn with Billy voluntarily holding her hand.

Schooled by Animals

Billy didn't like any of our animals. He had so much anger bottled up inside that he found it difficult to be gentle with anything. This concerned me because our house had always been a sanctuary for wounded and unwanted animals of every description. Over the years, we had raised or rescued scores of animals: raccoons, chicks, ducklings, goslings, cockatiels, pygmy goats, dogs, cats, even horses. The kids in the community called our small Florida ranch "Uncle Ben's Petting Farm." I became Billy's animal conscience, encouraging him to be more humane with the creatures under our care, but he preferred to observe our motley collection of animals from a comfortable distance.

Some of the most effective training Billy received came from the animals themselves. I recall one instance, while I ran to the house for something, when Billy decided to chase Buster, an ill-tempered horse we had just rescued. Mamma looked outside just in time to see Billy hit Buster with a heavy stick. I heard Mamma laughing at the same time I heard Billy's cries for help. I ran to the kitchen window and there was Billy, stick in hand, running as fast as he could barely in front of Buster's thundering hooves! Mamma knew him well enough, by then, that she wasn't too worried about his ability to escape harm.

Billy and I spent lots of time together. Our one common bond was a deep love of the wilderness. The two of us often went exploring in the woods and swamps behind our house. Once in awhile Billy went exploring alone. The first time he became excited about an animal was when a hungry fawn followed him home. He named the fawn Precious, and she was the first animal for which he learned to care. Precious would follow him anywhere and Billy loved the attention. Another time he brought home a baby otter and released him to grow up in our pond. The two of them often swam and played together. It was as if he learned from animals what he had difficulty learning from humans.

As Billy began to respond to kindness and discipline, the two forces that encircled our home, he was allowed to ride a horse. When I saw that he was careful, we started riding together, he on Nugget, a Palomino pony, and me on Angel, my white Shetland. We wandered through the Florida backlands, across streams, over woodland trails, and were often gone for hours at a time. That summer Billy became my best friend, my protector, my hero. Nothing will ever be able to remove my warm memories of those golden summer days.

One day we were riding through the Royal Trails Cypress Swamp when Billy dismounted in front of me and picked something up off of the trail. Cupped protectively in both hands he showed me a large, downy gray chick with a curved beak. Where did he come from? We both looked up. Towering far above us was a large osprey nest.

"We have to get him back up in his nest, Lara!" Billy hissed intently, failing to keep his voice to the whisper he was attempting. As usual, his tone reflected some degree of agitation, but it was tempered by a generous dose of empathy. "He'll die without his mother!"

"What should we do?" I asked, looking up at the smooth-barked tree that had no limbs for at least twenty-five feet, with absolutely nothing on which a climber might get a grip. Billy handed me the chick and rummaged through his ever-present backpack. He pulled out several discarded railroad spikes that we had gathered from the train track during our expedition that morning. Using a flat rock as a hammer, he pounded a couple of them into the tree at two foot intervals. Then, using the spikes as rungs, he climbed the tree, adding spikes as he climbed. Within a few minutes he was high enough to reach the limbs. He then returned for the chick. Gently placing it inside his shirt, he climbed back up. I always wondered what Billy whispered to that chick when he placed him back in his nest, but I knew what his tender actions meant; my brother was feeling secure enough in his own nest that he could afford to give another fledgling a chance. I can still put myself back under that tree, really looking up to my brother for the first time.

Helping the Wounded

A few weeks later, our neighbor phoned to say that he had discovered a wounded hawk. The bloody bullet wound on the red-tailed hawk's wing was, as Billy said in his charming drawl, "rat nasty." We wanted to help the bird, but Mandy and I had always favored the softer, more easily tamed animals. We were concerned about the hooked beak and sharp talons of this bird, but Billy leaned right down and picked up that mean-looking thing as if he was meant for the job. The neighbor gave Billy some fresh venison, and Mamma let him have an empty chicken coop for a cage.

Billy named the hawk Red. They became so attached to each other that Billy lost his fixation for guns because of the damage the bird had suffered. Billy would take Red outside for exercise every day by giving him a ride on his arm. Because Red could not fly while his wing was healing, Daddy rigged up a thick leather arm-protector so that the big bird could grip Billy's arm properly during their exercise time. I recall that once Daddy had to remove Red's talons from Billy's arm when he accidentally missed the protector after one of his first practice flights. Though Red had punctured Billy's arm, I was proud that my brother did not even give him a reprimand. Billy understood the recklessness that can hover in a wild heart.

Too soon, the day came for Red's release. Billy knew that the broken wing was healed; he had been expanding Red's test flights daily. I trotted behind Billy when he headed toward the barn that cloudless day and watched him toss Red high into the air. Red circled wide and returned to Billy. Billy threw him a little higher. Red flew farther, but once again returned to his familiar perch on Billy's arm. Finally, Billy climbed up on the roof of the barn, looked Red in the eye as if to say, "You're on your own, now, Red. I've done all I can to give you a second chance. Spread your wings! Go! Fly with the eagles!" Red took to the sky. We saw his brilliant tail disappear into the swamp.

After his success with Red, Billy took a more active role in helping wounded animals. He seemed to care a little more about family members, too, especially me. No neighborhood bullies would ever attempt to terrorize me if my protective brother was anywhere in the vicinity! As he matured, Billy became a skilled cowboy; he could talk horse language, and shoe any horse. The wilder the horse, the better he liked it. He took special pride in accomplishing feats with horses that others could not achieve.

Time to Fly

On Billy's wedding day, there were two things on his heart besides his beautiful bride. He took my parents aside and, with difficulty, confessed and apologized to them for his part in the mystery of the disappearing chickens. What he said next made all their long walks, their discipline, and heartache worth the effort.

"Mom and Dad," Billy said with emotion, "Without your love and care I would have spent my childhood in a juvenile detention facility. My wedding day would not have been as happy as it is. Thanks."

Billy was able to see that what my parents did for him was what he had done for Red; a sort of catch and release. Mamma and Daddy had performed the rescue, but I'd often been the first to witness evidence of his healing. I was thankful for the many adventures we had shared, pleased to watch his gift of tenderness develop, and delighted with his victories.

Tears came to my eyes when my brother kissed his bride. I would miss him, but it was time—time for him to fly.

All names in this story are pseudonyms.

If I Can Stop One Heart from Breaking

If I can stop one Heart from breaking,
I shall not live in vain;
If I can ease one Life the Aching,
Or cool one pain,
Or help one faltering Robin
Into his nest again,
I shall not live in vain.

—*Emily Dickenson*

The Raven and the Ring

W. A. Spicer and H. S. Menkel

"Behold, I set before you this day a blessing and a curse;
a blessing if ye obey the commandments of the Lord your God,
which I have commanded you this day;
and a curse if ye will not obey the commandments
of the Lord your God."

—Deuteronomy 10:26, 27

What was the poor peasant to do? It was midwinter, his family was starving, and they would soon be without a home. Two choices were open to Dobry, and only one would truly satisfy his honest heart.

Over the door of a certain house in Warsaw you will see an iron tablet with a very unique engraving in it. The house was built in the late 1700's by King Stanislaus for a peasant named Dobry. The engraving, along with a few sentences below it, tells this story.

Dobry's grandfather had trained a raven which he later set free. The raven flew in through the front door just as Dobry opened it to see if the landlord's hired men were coming to throw him, his wife and family, and their meager possessions out into the cold.

Dobry had been out of work for a time. Their money had been spent and they were now in arrears with the rent. He had gone to his landlord three times to appeal for mercy, but in vain. This was the last day they could remain in the home despite the fact that it was a very severe winter.

Answer to Prayer

Having heard very little about God, it seemed very strange to his wife when Dobry suggested that they ask this God to help them. He knelt with his family on the cold, hard floor and poured out his broken heart to the "God who answers prayer."

After he had finished his pleadings, his wife told him that she had a tablet on which she had copied some parts of a hymn her mother had sung a few times before her death. Shivering together, they filled the tiny cottage with these words; "Dein werk kann neimand hindern," which means

"Nothing Thy work suspending." The rest of the Lutheran pastor's old hymn went like this, "No foe can make Thee pause when Thou, Thine own defending, Dost understand their cause."

After singing a few verses, they sat down and said nothing to each other. Then Dobry spied the raven once again.

"He's got something in his beak!"

He took the object from the birds' grasp and held it up for closer examination. It was a beautiful and very expensive ring.

"God has answered our prayers," his wife said excitedly. "He sent us this valuable ring."

"But the ring isn't ours," Dobry said. "We don't know where the raven got it. Maybe we should see if we can find the owner."

"Dobry!" His wife almost shouted, "You just prayed for God to help us. Here is the answer! Let's sell the ring and get the money God sent us."

As Dobry looked at the emaciated faces of his little babies, and his crying wife, he tried to decide what was best to do.

"If we go and try to find out who lost the ring, we'll come back to find our things piled up in the snow," insisted his wife. "God sent us this ring. Let's sell it and live!"

Dobry was torn apart with mixed emotions. "If God did indeed send the ring, He could have just as easily sent the raven with a bag of gold," he told himself. "Was this the answer to my prayer?"

Difficult Decision

His mind was whirling. "I just cannot believe God would want me to have something that belonged to someone else."

He decided that it was better to be poor than to be a thief. So, he trudged the long snow-filled road to the heart of Warsaw to see the Christian minister.

When he had told the minister of his condition, his prayer, and of the raven, he showed him the ring. The minister stunned Dobry as he said,

"I believe I know who this ring belongs to. It looks exactly like one I saw King Stanislaus wearing. As you know, there aren't very many men around who can afford such an expensive ring."

Dobry thanked the minister and left. Once again his mind was flooded with all kinds of thoughts as well as fears. "If I had tried to sell it, I would have been arrested for stealing it!"

In the King's Palace

Dobry made his way to the magnificent palace to attempt to see the king. He knew that he must return the ring, even if the king thought he had stolen it.

After a long interrogation by several guards, Dobry was allowed to wait in a chamber while someone went to discuss it with the king. Dobry was terrified with the thought that the king wouldn't believe that a pet raven had brought the beautiful ring to him in his beak.

To Dobry's surprise, the king agreed to see him. Dobry was even more surprised to see the minister there, too.

"I have heard all about you, Dobry, I am proud that there is a man in my kingdom who would allow his family to be thrown out into the snow before he would keep my ring."

Dobry's heart was pounding faster than it ever had in all his life.

The king gave Dobry a large sum of money with which to pay his rent, buy food and clothing, and live on until summer came. Then came a surprise that almost took Dobry's life through disbelief.

The king ordered a new home built in Warsaw for Dobry and his family where he lived comfortably for the rest of his life.

The iron tablet with the unique engraving, of course, stands over Dobry's front door. The engraving? A picture of a raven with a ring in its beak.

A Mockingbird in Florida

A mockingbird in Florida at dawn begins to sing.
He floods my room with melody and sets me wondering
Can waking up to toil again be such a happy thing?

Incessant is his silver call. "Get up," he seems to trill,
"The sun is at the ocean's edge and soon your room will fill.
"Get up! Get up! Get up!" he cries. I mutter, "Oh, be still!"

Oh, little silver-throated bird, I cannot sing as you,
But when at last I quit my bed I've many tasks to do,
And it may be that I shall grieve before the day is through.

And I am sick with weariness and tired are my eyes;
The happiest man on earth is he who long in slumber lies,
And yet with joy you sing to me; "The dawn is in the skies."

I fancy you are right, and yet so oft I've waked to weep,
So oft I've risen but to lose the joys I'd longed to keep,
That grumblingly I quit my bed and say farewell to sleep.

But happy-hearted mockingbird that sings the morning in,
So much of happiness is here for human hearts to win
That we should be as glad as you to see the day begin.

—by Edgar Guest

Herkimer

with Jim Conway

"But they that wait upon the Lord shall renew their strength;
they shall mount up with wings as eagles; they shall run,
and not be weary; and they shall walk, and not faint."

—Isaiah 40:31

Pastor Jim Conway, first revealed his "real self" to an audience of Christian psychiatrists at the National Conference on the "Christian in Recovery" at La Marada, CA. His revelation is heart-rending, humble, and transparent; Jim learned from a pigeon how God moulds our damage into useable lessons so that, if we are willing to see life from a different perspective, and open up to the possibility of healing, even an injured bird can help us find our wings.

I'd like to tell you about a little bird that we adopted when I was pastoring a church on the edge of the University of Illinois. The little bird was a pigeon. We weren't sure if she was a he or he was a she but it had a broken leg and couldn't get around and had not yet learned to fly. A young couple in our church had taken it in, but the owner of their apartment building didn't want a pigeon in the apartment so he had asked the young couple to take it somewhere else. They elected us as the godparents of this pigeon. We called him Herkimer.

We cared for Herkimer, fed him with a bottle and gently kept track of the splinted leg. Pretty soon Herkimer got stronger and could walk around. We would go for walks in the evening with our dog, Misty. Herkimer would walk right along on the sidewalk behind us. He was part of the family and was enjoying this process.

Grounded

Now we realized that Herkimer was a bird, and that a bird should learn how to fly. So, when we thought it was the right time, we took the bird out into the back yard, held him up and just let go. There were a couple of flaps, and then down he went, into the soft grass. We did it again and again. Eventually Herkimer flapped his way to the edge of the lawn. We thought that Herkimer would soon be able to fly when we'd go out for walks. Yes, he would fly around for awhile, but he would land on the sidewalk and walk along right behind us. After all, we were his parents! We were the ones who taught him what to do. He was just modeling what he saw us doing. The thing to do, he thought, was to be walking on the ground, not flying around, although he had this capacity, too, and didn't understand why we couldn't fly! He was quite content just to walk with us.

There is a verse in Genesis that tells us "each brought forth after his own kind." That's exactly what happens in dysfunctional families. Dysfunctional parents bring forth dysfunctional children. Those dysfunctional children will generally marry dysfunctional mates. Those two dysfunctional people will then produce dysfunctional children and will automatically, unconsciously, train those children to be dysfunctional. So they will go out marry dysfunctional people who will raise dysfunctional children who will marry dysfunctional people. On and on it goes until finally someone says, "Hey, we gotta stop this!" And that is what recovery is all about;

stopping this process from going on endlessly—expanding and exploding. We've got to speak about our dysfunction and give other people permission to talk about their dysfunction.

Pursuit of Acceptance

I'm a Christian. In fact, I'm a pastor. I probably shouldn't be a dysfunctional person, but that's the kind of home I came from. I've tried all of my life to work harder, do more, be more perfect, so that maybe it wouldn't bother me to be dysfunctional. But, all my life, I didn't know it was abnormal to want to die. I thought everyone wished they could die. I thought everyone got up in the morning saying to themselves, "It would be really great if this was the day I could just *slip out*!"

I would say to my wife, "Tell me, Sally, why is it that you want to keep living when heaven is so wonderful and this life is such a hell-factory? Why keep on living?" And she would encourage me, but I don't remember a time when I didn't feel like an outsider, an alien. I felt as if God peopled the world with people, but somehow he brought in a strange alien person, me, into this world and I just didn't fit. I still feel like I don't fit—I still feel that I'm on the outside. So I keep trying harder. I'll write more books, maybe people will like me. I'll speak at more seminars, maybe people will like me. I'll help more people, maybe people will like me. Maybe I will finally like myself!

You know what happens at birth. The child comes first, then there is a period of waiting, and then the afterbirth comes. What I feel like is that when I was born, they somehow made a mistake—I had the feeling that they managed to throw out the baby and save the afterbirth, me. Yet, I am a person who is supposed to have all the pieces of life put together, but there is a wretchedness that has come out of my parental home that has been a giant pall over my life.

I came into a home where my father, the day after he was married, said to himself, "I married the wrong woman." But, because he was a Christian and was not going to get a divorce, he decided that he would stay with my mother. But he never went on to make the next decision. "I will try to make this marriage good!" He decided that the solution was to stay away from mother, avoid her, put her down, to try and kill her by proving that she was mentally incompetent; she would be locked up and he would be free. That's been going on all of their lives. They are still alive and the humiliation continues.

Somebody told my parents that having a child might heal the marriage. I was the kid that came along. "Heal this mess!" What a thing to dump on a child! "You're supposed to make it better, Jim!"

In my counseling practice I sometimes hear a child say to a father or mother, "Don't fight. Love Mommy. Love Daddy." That brings back memories of what I was trying to do as a child—attempting to somehow pull my parents together.

If you were born into a dysfunctional home, you were automatically reaching out and trying to bring about healing. Without knowing it, you were shouldering adult responsibilities even as a young child.

School Daze

In grade school I was a failure. All the way through school, I was a failure. Why? Because I was afraid of people. People would disappoint you. Remember that game that was popular back in the 60s and 70s—"Tell me the warmest room in your house"? Fun game. People would tell about some comfy place in their home. When my turn came, I would make up a story, just like everyone else. I knew they were lying, too. They were just pretending that there were comfortable places in their house. Surely, they were all just imagining that they were able to feel secure and content.

That's the attitude I had in school. Alone. Afraid. Suspicious. At recess time, I would stand in a corner of the playground, on an inside corner of the building, so I would be protected on all sides, and watch the other children play. Even in high school, I can remember my Spanish teacher calling me "The scared rabbit." I never caught on—all through school. I don't know how I managed to keep going through school, but before I finished my second doctorate my wife urged me to "at least learn to spell!" I still have not learned that. There was a big chunk of my education that I never achieved. Things like verbs, adverbs—I never figured them out! I know they are there and that I am probably using them, but I'm not sure what their names are or how to diagram them. My education had giant gaps because of my insecurity.

When I would sit down to take a test, my first reaction was, "You know you are going to fail this test because you've failed all the rest of them!" My reasoning powers were completely blocked from fear of failure. As a result I kept failing. Each of my teachers pushed me along until I was ultimately just pushed out of high school.

I am reminded of the story of the fellow who visited his psychiatrist, and after telling his problems and difficulties, the doctor said to him, "I want you to know that you shouldn't *feel* like you're a mess. You *are* a mess!" It wasn't that I was just *feeling* like a mess. I *was* a mess. My high school principle put his arm around my father's shoulder, while I was standing there, and said, "Mr. Conway, don't ever send this boy to college. You'll be wasting your money!"

When I was admitted to college (a thousand miles from home because none of the colleges any closer would admit me!), I was only admitted for six weeks. Not even a half a semester! Six weeks! And, if I didn't maintain a C average for 6 weeks, I was out! "C" average? I'd never make a "C" average! Somehow God would have to intervene.

Flight is a Choice

Fortunately, I had met God not long before I went to college. That was the first step in my recovery. God gave me some astounding, and very personal, promises: "Therefore because you are in Christ you are a new creation. Old things are in the process of passing away. All things are in the process of becoming new." From somewhere outside of myself, I sensed that I could believe God.

Watching Herkimer hobble along behind us, I began to understand how God must feel about me. I remain earthbound when I could, as the old hymn promises, "plant my feet on higher ground."

The day Herkimer flew, I was torn. He was, after all, only a pigeon! He'd not had the best start in life. I could not show him what to do, either. Yet, he had learned to fly in spite of my lack of wings.

Would I? Thankfully, there are some who have found their wings and are willing to help me fly.

The Snowbird

He sits in winter's sleet, and the snow is 'round his feet,
But he cares not for the cold;
For his little cheerful heart thinks the snow as fair a part
As the summer's green and gold.

On the branches bare and brown, with their crystals for a crown,
Sits the tiny winter bird;
In the dark and stormy days lightening the lonely ways
With his constant cheery word.

To his mission he is true; God has work for him to do—
With his happy song to cheer;
In his sweet life's simple speech lessons high and glad to teach
In the dark days of the year.

Oh, his little heart is strong, and he never thinks it wrong
That to him this lot is given;
Never envies birds that sing in the summer or the spring
Underneath a sunny heaven.

So he is a teacher sent with a lesson of content
To all spirits that are sad;
And his song, with richest freight, comes to all the desolate,
Bidding sorrow's self be glad.

"Wouldst thou choose thy time or way?"
seems the blithesome tune to say—
"God hath ordered these for thee;
Where thy life can praise him best he hath set thee; only rest
And his purpose thou shalt see."

Ye around whose life the snow lieth heavily and low,
Take a lesson from the bird;
As God giveth you to say, strive to charm the gloom away,
Whether heeded or unheard.

God hath singers, many a one, that can praise him in the sun,
As the happy cherubim;
But I think the songs they raise who are toilers in dark ways
Are a sweeter sound to him.

Not by outer joy and sweetness does he judge of life's completeness,
But by surer test of worth;
It may be he gives the grace of his heavens highest place
To the lowest of the earth.

—*Caroline Spencer*

Sparrow Hawk Summer

with Joel Nephew

The Lord shall help them and deliver them:
he shall deliver them from the wicked,
and save them, because they trust in him.

—Psalm 37:40

One special day it becomes clear to every child that it is time to learn to accept responsibility. What makes a child choose to become account-able, mature, responsible not only for themselves, but answerable to those within the circle of their influence? Sometimes the biggest lessons in life don't have many words attached to them. A child needs someone to model respectable values, show him how to sort through his hopes and dreams, help him build a firm foundation under the castles of childhood. The child who learns, by exercise and example, knows not only where to go, but how to rise, often against the current, above the things of time in order to achieve the heights for which they were created.

Good parents, and all great mentors, face the day that always comes too soon—the call to let go and stand by. Joel learned this valuable lesson early, when his father brought him a very special gift—two gifts, actually. Fortunate the lad whose mentor is his Dad!

The summer I turned thirteen, my father was hired to repair a barn. When the farmer and my father entered the barn, they saw a nest in the casing of the door that had to be repaired in order to function safely. Upon climbing up to inspect, Dad discovered two lively chicks. Knowing that their nest must be removed, he brought them home that evening.

"Look what I found today, Joel," he said, extending his work-calloused hands toward me.

"Whatchya gonna do with 'em, Dad?" I asked, hoping for the answer I wanted to hear.

"They're yours!"

I held out my hands. The chicks snuggled down. They felt warm. Their little hearts were beating fast, but they blinked up at me as if they trusted that I could make everything work together for their good. I had never before been entrusted with such a significant duty and was overwhelmed with a great sense of awe. The two chicks immediately became the center of my time and attention.

My father helped me construct a cage from an old barrel. Mom loaned me a small bowl from the kitchen for a watering dish. The birds were still too young to perch, so I shredded some newspaper and shaped a nest in the bottom of the cage and laid a branch crosswise knowing it wouldn't be long before they would need something on which to roost.

"What kind of birds are they, Dad?" I asked as we built the cage together. "What'll I feed 'em?"

"They are hawks, son. The farmer called them 'Sparrow Hawks' but you will probably not be able to tell their true colors in order to identify them until they have their adult plumage.

"What shall I feed them?"

"Hawks are meat-eaters, son. Ask your mother for some hamburger."

After warming the hamburger in the microwave I presented it to the chicks. They tore into it as if they were starving. They ate ravenously, making growling, gulping noises as they swallowed. After that first meal, whenever they heard me coming they would call to me and I would answer, "Time to eat!" They registered great enthusiasm at my approach.

Looking Upward

I checked out a library book about hawks and learned many facts I had not known, facts that I was pretty sure my friends didn't know either. When the birds were completely covered with their first feathers, I took them with me to church and school. They were a real hit wherever they went. When my friends would ask questions it made me feel important and humble all at the same time to be able to tell people about my hawks. I loved those birds with as much love as my thirteen-year-old heart could hold.

When my daily chores were finished, I would take their cage outside, open the door and let them play in the grass while I took turns letting my eyes wander from my baby hawks to the clouds overhead. I had always loved watching the clouds, but now I began to study them more seriously. Among the clouds, I saw birds soaring at great heights and began wondering about wind currents. Some birds barely moved their wings. What would it be like to fly? I knew that it had something to do with facing into the wind. Looking down at my chicks I wondered how they would learn to fly. Would they just automatically know about the currents that could lift them?

Looking Inward

By the end of July, their adult plumage had replaced every trace of chick fuzz. I contemplated building a larger cage so that I could keep them a little longer and they could still get exercise, but I knew, in my heart, that would not be the responsible thing to do. I didn't quite understand the term *responsible*—not because it was a particularly difficult concept, but because I sometimes chose not to understand. It seemed to me that Dad used that word a lot back in those days. It came up in nearly every conversation. Yes, I knew that, among other duties that fell to me, I needed to release my birds, but how would I feel when they rose to heights beyond my reach? Maybe they wouldn't even give me a backward glance. They wouldn't need me any more! I didn't want to think such big thoughts, but they just kept coming, like waves on the beach. I wanted my sparrow hawk summer to last forever.

I knew I must accept my parental responsibility; not only did I have to release my hawks; it was up to me to prepare them to succeed in the life they would live apart from me. I was an integral part of their ultimate freedom. They were used to me feeding them; how could I teach them to find their own food? For that matter, they couldn't fly, either! I redirected my focus; it was not responsible for me to just receive flattery, I needed to be giving more attention to training these birds to be independent. It was the responsible thing to do.

Into the Wind

With the chicks clinging to my fingers—one on the left hand and one on the right—I walked down our long driveway, slowly raising and lowering my arms. The chicks flapped their wings. Over the next few days, I gradually increased ground speed. Their wings flapped faster. The chicks joyfully participated in the exercise, but they would not release their grip. If their wing muscles were growing in proportion to their talon strength, they would have to fly soon or I'd have to start wearing hand and arm protection. I smile as I envision the image the neighbors may have had of a WW1 Ace, both engines on full throttle as my 'sparrow hawk biplane' roared through the neighborhood.

My chicks, now full grown, at last started finding their own bugs, but I had just about decided that they were stuck to me forever, when suddenly it happened. I was approaching home after a particularly invigorating pre-flight exercise when I gave my hands an extra hard upward thrust. Like the Blue Angels in formation, my hawks took off for their first solo flight!

They circled behind the house, just as I had envisioned. I had already decided I wouldn't follow them if they did fly away. I would release them with whatever dignity I could muster. I did, however, crane my neck as they disappeared from view. That's when I heard the commotion—a loud whirring noise. I looked up just in time.

On the lookout for potential air enemies, Sergeant Robin and his first mate, nesting among the spruce trees in our back yard, had spotted two enemy war hawks headed for their babies. My birds were being dive-bombed! They were headed straight back toward me—yelling at the top of their lungs in their loudest hawk language—"Wing Man! Hey, Wing Man! Over here! Prepare landing pad!"

They landed on me, one on each shoulder, quickly tucking their heads up tightly behind my ears! Those dive-bombing robins took one look at my chicks' defense strategy and made a remarkable about-face in midair. My heart felt like it would burst right through my rib cage! I was so proud to be their protector. They came to me, by choice, for protection, just like I came to my Dad when things weren't going so well for me.

Far Horizons

The chicks stretched their flights for a few more days until they were returning only at nightfall. I scanned the horizon for a long time when the hawks finally left my world to live in their own. My heart hurt, but, by then, I was a little more prepared for them to become independent. I found myself scanning the horizon at sunset for several weeks, thinking about how much I had learned from them. They surely owed me nothing. I often said a prayer for them, not unlike the prayers my father prayed for me when I left for college.

Through the years, I've wondered about my hawks, especially when some challenge I face makes me wish for a safe hiding place. Whenever I feel unequal to the call of true responsibility, those little hawks come to mind and I still feel the soft warmth of their heads pressing against the back of my ears that wonderful day when they came back to me for protection. They trusted me. As a parent, now, I think of the heavy responsibility on my shoulders to be there for my children, encouraging them to climb ever higher, to be all that God has called them to be, holding them up in prayer.

No matter how fiercely the currents of trouble may blow, remembering how my hawks came to me for protection has become a living picture of how my heavenly Father cares for me. Just as I prepared my chicks to face life, just so my parents and the Lord prepared me to face life as a representative of the realms of glory. Knowing that I am on His side, I am encouraged, once more, to rise above the bonds of earth and experience new heights. And He is always there for me.

Like the warm, golden memory of my "Sparrow Hawk Summer," He is always with me.

Bird Nests

What a wonder the world is
For a little girl of five
At the June time of the year,
And so good to be alive,
With the meadows to explore,
Seeking bird nests near and far,
And a dad of forty-four
Who can show her where they are!

Every evening after tea
We go wandering about
To the nests which we have found,
Where the little birds are out.
And we tiptoe hand in hand
To a certain lovely crest
Where delightedly we stand
At a killdeer's curious nest.

And a meadow-lark we know
With five babies of her own!
What a wonder world it is
And what miracles are shown!
She can scarcely stay for tea—
How she bolts her pudding through,
With so much she wants to see
And so much she wants to do!

So we hurry out of doors
And excitedly we race
To the mother meadow-lark
And the killdeer's secret place
And we talk of God who made
All the birds and trees and flowers,
And we whisper, half afraid:
"What a wonder world is ours!"

—by Edgar Guest

Calling the Eagles

with Darrell Lindgren

Doth the eagle mount up at thy command...?

—Job 39:27

*D*arrell is one of those deep, gentle souls that one counts it a privilege to have as a personal friend. When he mentioned that God had used birds to bring him to the cross, my inquiry resulted in the telling of a most inspirational story. He, like Albert Einstein, has discovered that we have the choice of living one of two ways: 1) as if there are no miracles, or 2) as if everything is! Here is how Darrell became convinced that there is no such thing as coincidence.

God was working with me when I was, as yet, not working with Him. I think He does that with a lot of us. I first began to sense that He was trying to get my attention before my life fell apart, but I wasn't quite willing to listen. Life was not nearly as bad as it would get before I would listen to Him more carefully. Life, however, had warned me that I needed to at least begin to consider seeking counsel or I would be facing some music I was not prepared to hear.

I began reading self help books, trying to meditate, and exploring New Age philosophies. One of the challenges to which I was exposed was the idea of "coincidence". Could I, just by thinking, bring about a certain happening? As I considered the possibilities of why certain phenomenon occur, I began to pay close attention to coincidences manifesting themselves in my own life.

I'd think to myself, "I'd like to see an eagle." Not too long thereafter, lo and behold, I would see an eagle! What a coincidence! Like I say, though, God was working with me on this. He actually let me think, for awhile, that I had something to do with it. Whenever I'd ask to see one, He would send me one.

One quiet summer day I was standing in front of the glass doors that open onto my patio while I considered this fascinating idea of "coincidence". The thought flashed into my mind that I would like to see the large hawk whose territory was near my home. Within a mere fraction of a second, the big hawk crossed in front of my patio and hovered there, right in front of me, about 15 feet above the ground! The wind currents are often such, in that particular place, that he could hover with little effort. Slowly and majestically, as if he knew I was watching him, he worked his way out into the field, maintaining his hovering pattern about 15 feet above the ground until I could no longer see him. Tears streamed down my face. I knew, beyond a shadow of doubt, in that moment, that I had no power within me to cause this bird to listen to my mental commands. This was God's doing. And the bigger message was that God was hearing me.

Not long after this hawk incident, a powerful development occurred in my life that I had feared might be coming. I could no longer ignore it. I was devastated. I could not fix it. Nothing helped: not my self help books, not New Age philosophies, no positive thinking, absolutely nothing lifted me. I was at rock bottom. There was nothing to do but surrender. The peace was overwhelming.

At sunset one evening, while studying for baptism, I looked out the same window through which I had seen the wished-for-hawk. There, on the western horizon, was the largest bird anyone had ever seen! His wingspan had to have measured no less than 5 miles across! He had rays of sunshine, at least 40 rays, streaming through his wings. It was spectacular—stunning. It was so absolutely perfect in every detail. It was by far the most beautiful cloud formation I have ever seen, and it hovered there for several minutes.

If you come to my house I can show you the horizon where this majestic phenomenon appeared. I cannot think of that evening without the intense conviction stealing over me that it was a life-changing experience with God Himself. I no longer ask Him to send me eagles, or hawks. I don't need them any more. I have but to close my eyes and recall the great bird I saw in the clouds to know I am under the care of a mightier power than any philosophy or principality that flies beneath the clouds of heaven.

With the Eagle

His eye
Sweeps all the sky,
As hard he grips the rock.
Storm's ice-clad brood that round him flock
But blow the fires of his undaunted breast,
And forth he fares in ecstasy of quest.
Still up he goes, to proudly fling
His own against the thunder's wing.

O Eagle of the mighty heart,
Give me of what Thou art:
Breed in my soul Thy lofty air,
That it may nobly dare,
And with unconquerable will
Face every darkest ill.

—*Edward Robson Taylor (1838–1923)*

Wings of Life

by Yellowstone Park Rangers

He shall cover you with His feathers,
and under His wings you shall take refuge.

—Psalm 91:4, NKJV

In 1988, Yellowstone National Park was ravaged by fire. I had seen the wonders of the park several times and it pained me to hear of the devastation. When I recently revisited the park, I did see the damage, but I was encouraged by the new growth. This story comes from the still-warm ashes of that fire, an example of the spirit of self-sacrificing love that speaks of a Creator who placed that little spark of self-sacrificing care that man might mistakenly label as mere instinct.

After a forest fire in Yellowstone National Park, forest rangers began their trek up a mountain to assess the inferno's damage. One ranger found a bird literally petrified in ashes, perched statuesquely on the ground at the base of a tree. Somewhat sickened by the eerie sight, he knocked over the bird with a stick. When he gently struck it, three tiny chicks scurried from under their dead mother's wings.

The loving mother, keenly aware of impending disaster, had carried her offspring to the base of the tree and had gathered them under her wings, instinctively knowing that the toxic smoke would rise. She could have flown to safety but had refused to abandon her babies. When the blaze arrived and the heat had scorched her small body, the mother had remained steadfast. Because she had been willing to die, those under the cover of her wings could live.

Does the lesson sound familiar—something you might have read about the protective love of God? There is a fire-storm coming, but those who have learned where to hide, beneath the shelter of His wings, will find safety in the time of trouble. How would it feel to snuggle safely beneath the shelter of His care today? Knowing we are loved this much makes a big difference!

Under His Wings

Under His wings I am safely abiding;
Though the night deepens and tempests are wild,
Still I can trust Him, I know He will keep me,
He has redeemed me and I am His child.

Under His wings,
Under His wings,
Who from His love can sever?
Under His wings my soul shall abide,
Safely abide forever.

Under His wings what a refuge in sorrow,
How the heart yearningly longs for its rest!
Often when earth has no balm for my healing,
There I find comfort and there I am blest.

Under His wings, O what precious enjoyment!
There will I hide till life's trials are o'er;
Sheltered protected, no evil can harm me;
Resting in Jesus I'm safe ever more.

—*W. O. Cushing*

The Refuge

by J. H. Merle D'Aubigné

*"God who prepares His work through ages,
accomplishes it by the weakest instruments
when His time is come."*

—D'Aubigné

The story behind a great hymn has always been as inspiring to me as the actual lyrics of the song, and I know of no story more uplifting than the "coincidence" surrounding one of my favorite melodies, "Jesus Lover of My Soul," penned by Charles Wesley in 1740. As with all of his hymns, Wesley so blessedly adheres to such strict meter and rhyme scheme that the song is easily pressed into memory. The story of the song elegantly couples with the message, embedding itself with an unforgettable impact.

There is an interesting incident mentioned in the life of Charles Wesley, which led to the writing of one of his best known hymns.

One summer day, Mr. Wesley was sitting by an open window, looking out over the beautiful fields. Presently, a little bird flitting about in the sunshine attracted his attention. Just then, a hawk came sweeping down toward the little bird. The poor thing, very much frightened, was darting here and there, trying to find some place of refuge. In the bright, sunny air, in the leafy trees, or the green fields, there was no hiding place from the fierce grasp of the hawk.

Seeing the open window and the man sitting by it, the bird flew in its terror toward it, and with fast-beating heart and quivering wing, found refuge in Mr. Wesley's bosom. He sheltered it from the threatening danger, and saved it from a cruel death. But there is more to the story.

Mr. Wesley was at the time suffering severe trials, and was feeling the need of a refuge in his own time of trouble, as much as the trembling little bird, that nestled in his bosom. So he took up his pen and wrote the beautiful hymn recorded in full on the next page.

(From *Signs of the Times*, September 1, 1881)

Jesus, Lover of My Soul

Jesus, lover of my soul,
Let me to Thy bosom fly,
While the waves of trouble roll,
While the tempest still is high;
Hide me, O my Savior hide!
Till the storm of life is past;
Safe into the haven guide
O receive my soul at last!

Other refuge have I none,
Hangs my helpless soul on Thee;
Leave, O leave me not alone!
Still support and comfort me;
All my trust in Thee is stayed,
All my help from Thee I bring;
Cover my defenseless head
With the shadow of Thy wing.

Thou, O Christ, art all I want
More than all in Thee I find;
Raise the fallen, cheer the faint,
Heal the sick, and lead the blind.
Just and holy is Thy name,
I am all unrighteousness;
Vile and full of sin I am,
Thou art full of truth and grace.

Plenteous grace with Thee is found—
Grace to pardon all my sin.
Let the healing streams abound,
Make and keep me pure within.
Thou of life the fountain art,
Freely let me take of Thee;
Spring thou up within my heart,
Rise to all eternity!

—*Charles Wesley*

Crowned

Blessed [is] the man that endureth temptation:
for when he is tried, he shall receive the crown of life,
which the Lord hath promised to them that love him.

—James 1:12

*D*ennis hadn't always practiced his Christianity as he should have, so he had some serious questions about his acceptance with God. He'd had difficulty making wise choices, upholding the good, separating himself from bad influences. As he drove through the everlasting hills of Oklahoma on his way to work that day, he was considering how he had denied God. Like Peter of old, he couldn't help but wonder if God really loved him and if there could ever be a place in His kingdom for such a wretch. He did not know of the fatal danger that lurked a few minutes ahead of him, and it was not until much later that he would come to realize what a miraculous lesson of assurance God had given him that day; not just about His selfless love, but about celestial timing and, unmistakable, heaven-sent defense. It was unthinkable that a tiny bird could shield a grown man from a psychopath whose "button" had innocently been pressed because of some simple paperwork...

Dennis drove to his plumbing and heating supply business recounting the blessings of being his own boss. His books were showing a profit. His wife had just finished bringing the accounting up-to-date. Yes, it had been a good year. He was not a singer, but he found himself humming softly to himself about how God is so good, how He answers prayer, and…yes, how He is coming soon. His conscience was pricked; he was a Christian, and he knew the Lord was coming; he also knew that there was a definite deficit on the heavenly ledger opposite his name.

He had made unwise choices, even recently, that went against his conscience. He knew better. Why did he always end up stepping down from principle when he should be taking a firm stand for truth? In spite of his repentance, it was difficult for Dennis to feel his acceptance with God. Yes, he had asked forgiveness, but he suspected he would fail again, miserably. He was doing better, but doubts and fears still prevented him from the spiritual accomplishments he desired to achieve. Today he was feeling more "connected" than usual; he had spent time in the Word, and had prayed for divine guidance and protection before leaving home.

Happy Thoughts

It was a beautiful summer day. The blackberries were ripening. Would Heidi have some cobbler ready for supper? He was grateful for her love of their country home and how she kept everything in order. She had even managed to get those pesky W-9 forms mailed out last week. She was a good wife. She'd sent him off to work with his favorite peanut butter sandwiches and a piece of her delicious apple pie leftover from their Sabbath meal. It was good to be alive.

Then his thoughts turned to his co-workers, and after reviewing the list, his smile broadened as he considered Bouncer, a mammoth of a man, a regular forklift, who had absolutely no hint of people skills. He had stalked into the office a year earlier, with a dirty, threadbare t-shirt stretched tightly across his massive chest. What he lacked in cleanliness contrasted sharply with his shiny head, always shaved smooth so that it shone like chrome. Bouncer didn't talk much, so Dennis didn't know anything about his background, but he suspected a psychotic condition resulting from trauma. Except for those times when he would walk away from an assignment with his fists tightened, Bouncer had been a good employee, always ready to lift a load that would strain two average men.

Mondays were generally busy, so Dennis pulled his pickup into a parking spot at the back of the building so as to leave more spaces available for customers to park out in front. He gave Old Blue a pat on her front fender as he headed down the alley between the parking lot and the back of the building, ready to tackle the first job of the week. Before he reached the end of the alley, who should loom before him but Bouncer himself, and, because of the threatening set of his jaw, he appeared to loom even larger than usual. Dennis kept his voice cheerful.

Fearful Encounter

"Morning, Bouncer," he greeted the colossal creature blocking his progress. No answer.

"How are you today?" Still no answer, just a steady glare from those cold blue eyes.

"What can I do for you?"

Bouncer's nostrils flared as he struggled to control his words, "Told you not to send me a W-9."

"Oh? Hmmm, we did catch up our paperwork so that the employees could send in their tax returns. Yours was mailed out, too…with the rest… I guess."

"Don't *do* taxes. Told you that."

"Oh, right."

Bouncer tightened his fists and flexed his biceps. Dennis took a step backwards and sent up an emergency prayer.

Lord, what should I do? Please protect me! Help!

At that very instant, Dennis heard a whirring sound above his head. Bouncer's mouth flew open, and a look of absolute terror replaced his fury. He began backing up with one arm in front of his face as if to shield himself from some dreadful weapon of mass destruction.

Dennis felt something land on his head. His protective reflexes kicked in; was it a snake? A tarantula? A scorpion? He swiped his hand quickly across the top of his head. It hit something that quickly moved beyond his reach. Again he heard the whirring sound before "it" landed on his head again. A bird! That was fine with Dennis, especially considering the effect it had on Bouncer who was running with total abandon across the parking lot, serious about escaping with his life! It seemed his own fear had transferred to Bouncer and multiplied itself a hundredfold.

Deliverance

Had it not been such a serious situation, Dennis might have laughed aloud to see such a generous hunk of humanity attempting to overcome inertia. No more fists—Bouncer's hands were "flat out," pumping like drivers on a steam engine. He was glancing backward at regular intervals to ascertain his safety. He fell hard against his pickup to stop his momentum, jerked open the door, quickly arranged his enormous bulk behind the steering wheel, slammed the door shut and tore out of the parking lot.

"I wish I could have seen my benefactor," Dennis says through the smile he found that day. "But as soon as Bouncer was out of the parking lot, my little angel flew away. Judging by the look on Bouncer's face, the bird might have appeared to him as a giant Chinese Fighting Pheasant with colossal claws and a razor-sharp beak, but to me he just felt like one of a hundred plain little brown sparrows that lived in the big cottonwood grove behind the shop.

Pattern of Love

"I can still feel those tiny little feet dancing on my head whenever I am tempted to doubt God's custom-made love. I can so easily sense the reality of His nearness, now. One day soon, if I am faithful, Jesus' nail-scarred hands will place a circlet of gold on my head in the exact location that a little guardian angel once tattooed an indelible pattern of God's protective love.

"I never saw Bouncer again. He didn't even come back for his pay! I have wondered if he ever sent in that W-9. I'm grateful to him because that experience changed my life. Beyond any shadow of doubt, I knew that God loved me, personally—enough to send a little angel to cover my head at the precise time that I desperately needed coverage. Not a hair was harmed. Coincidence? Not a chance! I have never had a bird land on my head since that day, nor have I heard of any such thing happening to anyone else in the vicinity of that cottonwood grove!"

All names in this story are pseudonyms.

My Religion

My religion's lovin' God, who made us, one and all,
Who marks, no matter where it be, the humble sparrow's fall;
An' my religion's servin' Him the very best I can
By not despisin' anything He made, especially man!
It's lovin' sky an' earth an' sun an' birds an' flowers an' trees,
But lovin' human beings more than any one o' these.

If God can mark the sparrow's fall, I don't believe He'll fail
To notice us an' how we act when doubts an' fears assail;
I think He'll hold what's in our hearts above what's in our creeds,
An' judge our religion here by our recorded deeds;
An' since man is God's greatest work since life on earth began,
He'll get to heaven, I believe, who helps his fellowman.

—Edgar Guest

The Flight of the Red Tail

by Penny Porter

If I could wish for my life to be perfect, it would be tempting,
but I would have to decline,
for life would no longer teach me anything.

—Allyson Jones

The hawk hung from the sky, as though suspended from an invisible web, its powerful wings outstretched—motionless. It was like watching a magic show—until, suddenly, the spell was shattered by a shotgun blast from the car behind us.

Startled, I lost control of my pickup. Careening wildly, it slid sideways across the gravel shoulder until we stopped inches short of a barbed wire fence. My heart hammered in my chest as a car raced past us, the steel muzzle of a gun sticking out the window. As long as I live, I shall never forget the gleeful smile on the face of the boy who'd pulled that trigger.

"Geez, Mom. That scared me!" My son Scott, 14, was sitting beside me. Then his face clouded. "I thought he was shooting at us! But look! He shot that hawk!"

While driving back to the ranch from Tucson along Arizona's Interstate 10, we had been marveling at a magnificent pair of red-tailed hawks swooping low over the Sonoran Desert. Cavorting and diving at breath-taking speeds over the yucca and cholla cacti, the beautiful birds mirrored each other in flight.

Suddenly, one hawk changed its course and soared skyward where it hovered for an instant over the interstate as though challenging its mate to join in the fun. But the blast from the gun put an end to their play, converting the moment into an explosion of feathers dashed against the red and orange sunset.

Horrified we watched the red-tail spiral earthward, jerking and spinning straight into the path of an on-coming 18-wheeler. Air brakes screeched. But it was too late. The truck struck the bird, hurling it onto the medial strip.

Scott and I jumped from the pickup and ran to the spot where the stricken bird lay. Because of the hawk's size, we decided it was probably a male. He was on his back, a shattered wing doubled beneath him, the powerful beak open, and round, yellow eyes wide with pain and fear. The talons on his left leg had been ripped off. And, where the brilliant fan of tail feathers had once gleamed like a kite of burnished copper against the southwestern sky, only one red feather remained.

"We gotta do something, Mom," said Scott.

"Yes," I murmured. "We've got to take him home."

For once I was glad Scott was in style with the black leather jacket he loved because when he reached for him, the terrified hawk lashed out with his one remaining weapon—a hooked beak as sharp as an ice pick. To protect himself, Scott threw the jacket over the bird, wrapped him firmly and carried him to the pickup. When I reached for the keys still hanging in the ignition, the sadness of the moment doubled. From somewhere high in the darkening sky, we heard the plaintive, high-pitched cries of the other hawk.

"What will that one do now, Mom?" Scott asked.

"I don't know," I answered softly. "I've always heard they mate for life."

At the ranch we tackled our first problem; restraining the flailing hawk without getting hurt ourselves. Wearing welding gloves, we laid him on some straw inside an orange crate and slid the slats over his back.

Once the bird was immobilized we removed splinters of bone from his shattered wing, and then tried bending the wing where the main joint had been. It would only fold half way. Through all this pain, the hawk never moved. The only sign of life was an occasional rising of the third lid over the fear-glazed eyes.

Wondering what to do next, I telephoned the Arizona-Sonora Desert Museum. When I described the plight of the red-tailed hawk, the curator was sympathetic. "I know you mean well," he said, "but euthanasia is the kindest thing."

"You mean destroy him?" I asked, leaning down and gently stroking the auburn-feathered bird secured in the wooden crate on my kitchen floor.

"He'll never fly again with a wing that badly injured," he explained, "and even if he could, he'd starve to death. Hawks need their claws as well as their beaks to tear up food. I'm really sorry."

As I hung up, I knew he was right.

"But the hawk hasn't even had a chance to fight," Scott argued.

Fight for what? I wondered. To huddle in a cage, never to fly again?

Suddenly, with the blind faith of youth, Scott made the decision for us. "Maybe, by some miracle, he'll fly again someday." he said. "Isn't it worth the try?"

So began a weeks-long vigil during which the bird never moved, ate, or drank. We forced water into his beak with a hypodermic syringe, but the pathetic creature just lay there staring, unblinking, scarcely breathing. Then came the morning when the eyes of the red-tail were closed.

"Mom, he's...dead!" Scott pressed his fingers beneath the matted feathers. I knew he was searching, praying for a heartbeat. The memory of a speeding car, and a smiling boy with a gun in his hands returned to haunt me.

"Maybe some whiskey," I said. It was a last resort, a technique we had used before to coax an animal to breathe. We pried open the beak and poured a teaspoon of the liquid down the hawk's throat. Instantly his eyes flew open, and his head fell into the water bowl in the cage.

"Look at him, Mom! He's drinking!" Scott said, with tears sparkling in his eyes.

By nightfall the hawk had eaten several strips of round steak dredged in sand to ease digestion. The next day, his hands still shielded in welding gloves, Scott removed the bird from the crate and carefully wrapped his good claw around a fireplace log where he teetered and swayed until the talons locked in. As Scott let go of the bird, the good wing flexed slowly into flight position, but the other was rigid, protruding from its shoulder like a boomerang. We held our breath until the hawk stood erect.

The creature watched every move we made, but the look of fear was gone. He was going to live. Now, would he learn to trust us?

With Scott's permission, his three-year-old sister, Becky, named our visitor Hawkins. We put him in a chain-link dog-run ten feet high and open at the top. There he'd be safe from bobcats, coyotes, raccoons and lobos. In one corner of the pen, we mounted a manzanita limb four inches from the ground. A prisoner of his injuries, the crippled bird perched there day and night, staring at the sky, watching, listening, and waiting.

As fall slipped into winter, Hawkins began molting. Despite a diet of meat, lettuce, cheese and eggs he lost most of his neck feathers. More fell from his breast, back, and wings, revealing scattered squares of soft down. Pretty soon he looked like an old bald-headed man huddled in a patchwork quilt.

"Maybe some vitamins will help," said Scott. "I'd hate to see him lose that one red tail feather. "He looks kinda funny as it is."

The vitamins did seem to help. A luster appeared on the wing feathers, and we imagined a glimmer on that tail feather too.

In time, Hawkins' growing trust blossomed into affection. We delighted in spoiling him with treats like bologna and beef jerky soaked in sugar water. Soon, the hawk whose beak was powerful enough to snap the leg bone of a jack rabbit or crush the skull of a desert rat had mastered the touch of a butterfly. Becky fed him with her bare fingers.

Hawkins loved to play games. His favorite was tug-of-war. With an old sock gripped tightly in his beak and one of us pulling on the other end, he always won, refusing to let go, even when Scott lifted him into the air and swung him around like a bolo. Becky's favorite game was ring-around-a-rosy. She and I held hands and circled Hawkins' pen, while his eyes followed until his head turned 180 degrees. He was actually looking at us backward!

We grew to love Hawkins. We talked to him. We stroked his satiny feathers. We had saved and tamed a wild creature. But now what? Shouldn't we return him to the sky, to the world where he belonged?

Scott must have been wondering the same thing, even as he carried his pet around on his wrist like a proud falconer. One day he raised Hawkins's perch to 20 inches, just over the bird's head. "If he has to struggle to get up on it, he might get stronger," he said.

Noticing the height difference, Hawkins assessed the change from every angle. He scolded and clacked his beak. Then, he jumped—and missed, landing on the concrete, hissing pitifully. He tried again and again with the same result. Just as we thought he'd give up, he flung himself up at the limb, grabbing first with his beak, then his claw, and pulled. At last he stood upright.

"Did you see that, Mom?" said Scott. "He was trying to use his crippled wing. Did you see?"

"No," I said. But I'd seen something else, the smile on my son's face. I knew he was still hoping for a miracle.

Each week after that, Scott raised the perch a little more, until Hawkins sat proudly at four feet. How pleased he looked—puffing himself up grandly and preening his ragged feathers. But four feet was his limit. He could jump no higher.

Spring brought warm weather and birds: doves, quail, road runners and cactus wrens. We thought Hawkins would enjoy all the chirping and trilling. Instead we sensed sadness in our little hawk. He scarcely ate, ignoring invitations to play, preferring to sit with his head cocked, listening.

One morning we found him perched with his good wing extended, the crippled one quivering helplessly. All day he remained in this position, a piteous rasping cry coming from his throat. Finally we saw what was troubling him: high in the sky over his pen, another red-tail hovered.

His mate? I asked myself. How could it be? We were at least 30 miles from where we'd found Hawkins, far beyond a hawk's normal range. Had his mate somehow followed him here? Or through some secret of nature, far beyond our understanding, did she simply know where he was?

"What will she do when she realizes he can't fly?" Scott asked.

"I imagine she'll get discouraged and leave," I said sadly. "We'll just have to wait and see."

Our wait was brief. The next morning Hawkins was gone. A few broken feathers and bits of down littered his pen—silent clues to a desperate struggle.

Questions tormented us. How did he get out? The only possibility was that he'd simply pulled himself six feet up the fence, grasping the wire first with his beak, then his one good claw. Next he must have fallen ten feet to the ground.

How would he survive? He couldn't hunt. Clinging to his perch and a strip of meat at the same time with one claw had proven nearly impossible. What about the coyotes and bobcats? Our crippled hawk would be an easy prey. We were heartsick.

A week later, however, there was Hawkins perched on the log pile by our kitchen door. His eyes gleamed with a brightness I'd never seen before. And his beak was open! "He's hungry!" I shouted. The bird snatched a package of bologna from Scott's hand and ate greedily.

Finished, Hawkins hopped awkwardly to the ground and prepared to leave. We watched as he lunged, floated, and crashed in short hops across the pasture, one wing flapping mightily, the other a useless burden. Journeying in front of him, his mate swooped back and forth, scolding and whistling her encouragement until he reached the temporary safety of a mesquite grove.

Hawkins returned to be fed throughout the spring. Then one day, instead of taking his food, he shrank back, an unfamiliar squawk coming from his throat. We talked to him softly like we used to do, but suddenly he struck out with his beak. The hawk that had trusted us for nearly a year was now afraid. I knew he was ready to return to the wild.

As the years passed, we occasionally saw a lone red-tail gliding across our pastures, and my heart would leap with hope. Had Hawkins somehow survived? And if he hadn't, was it worth the try to keep him alive as we did?

Nine years later, when Scott was 23, he met an old friend in Phoenix who had lived near our ranch. "You won't believe this, Scott," he said, "But I think I saw your hawk roosting in a scrub oak down by the wash when I was home for Christmas. He was all beat up, broken wing just like Hawkins."

"You gotta go take a look, Mom."

The next day I drove north until the dirt roads became zigzagging cattle trails and finally no trails at all. When a barricade of thorny mesquite trees and wild rose bushes stopped me, it was time to walk. Finally an opening through the maze led me down to a twisting, sandy river bed; a paradise for lizards, toads, tarantulas, snakes, and small rodents of the desert. It was also an ideal feeding ground for a hawk.

Flanked by the spiny overgrowth on the banks above, I walked for hours, but saw no trace of Hawkins. But hope plays such tricks on the eyes, ears, and mind; I confess there were moments when the rustling of leaves, the clumps of mistletoe swaying on high branches, and the shifting shadows against gnarled tree trunks both kindled my fantasies and snuffed them out in a single second. Finding him was too much to hope for.

It was getting cold when I sensed I was being watched. Then, all of a sudden I was looking straight into the eyes of a large female red-tail. Roosting in a mesquite less than 15 feet away, she was perfectly camouflaged by the autumn foliage surrounding her.

Could this magnificent creature have been Hawkins' mate? I wondered. I wanted so much to believe she was, to tell Scott I had seen the bird that had cared for her mate, scavenged for his food and kept him safe. But how could I be sure?

Then I saw him!

On a low branch, beneath the great dark shadow of the larger bird, hunched a tattered little hawk. When I saw the crooked wing, the proud bald head and withered claw, my eyes welled with tears. This was a magic moment: a time to reflect on the power of hope. A time to pray for the boy with a gun. A time to bless the boy who had faith.

Alone in this wild, unaltered place, I learned the power of believing, for I had witnessed a miracle.

"Hawkins," I murmured, longing to stroke the ragged feathers, but daring only to circle around him. "Is it really you?"

My answer came when the yellow eyes followed my footsteps until he was looking at me backward, and the last rays of sunlight danced on—one red feather.

Then, finally, I knew—and, best of all, my son would know. It had been worth the try.

The Exposed Nest

You were forever finding some new play.
So when I saw you down on hands and knees
In the meadow, busy with the new-cut hay,
Trying, I thought, to set it up on end,
I went to show you how to make it stay,
If that was your idea, against the breeze,
And, if you asked me, even help you pretend
To make it root again and grow afresh.
But 'twas no make-believe with you today,
Nor was the grass itself your real concern,
Though I found your hand full of wilted fern,
Steel-bright June-grass, and blackening heads of clover.
'Twas a nest full of young birds on the ground
The cutter-bar had just gone champing over
(Miraculously without tasting flesh)
And left defenseless to the heat and light.
You wanted to restore them to their right
Of something interposed between their sight
And too much world at once—could means be found.
The way the nest-full every time we stirred
Stood up to us as to a mother-bird
Whose coming home has been too long deferred,
Made me ask would the mother-bird return
And care for them in such a change of scene?
And might our meddling make her more afraid?
That was a thing we could not wait to learn.
We saw the risk we took in doing good,
But dared not spare to do the best we could
Though harm should come of it; so built the screen
You had begun, and gave them back their shade.
All this to prove we cared. Why is there then
No more to tell? We turned to other things.
I haven't any memory—have you?—
Of ever coming to the place again
To see if the birds lived the first night through,
And so at last to learn to use their wings.

—Robert Frost

TEACH Services, Inc.
P U B L I S H I N G
www.TEACHServices.com ● (800) 367-1844

We invite you to view the complete
selection of titles we publish at:
www.TEACHServices.com

We encourage you to write us
with your thoughts about this,
or any other book we publish at:
info@TEACHServices.com

TEACH Services' titles may be purchased in
bulk quantities for educational, fund-raising,
business, or promotional use.
bulksales@TEACHServices.com

Finally, if you are interested in seeing
your own book in print, please contact us at:
publishing@TEACHServices.com

We are happy to review your manuscript at no charge.

CPSIA information can be obtained
at www.ICGtesting.com
Printed in the USA
BVHW030341231118
533754BV00002B/393/P